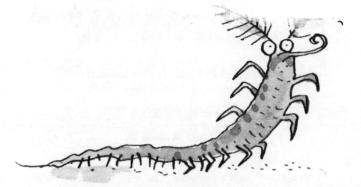

THIS BOOK BELONGS TO:

FOR LARRY HAYES – I WISH YOU'D KNOWN THESE
SECRETS WHEN YOU WERE YOUNG. YOU'D BE
WORLD PRESIDENT BY NOW. – L.H.

FOR MY TALENTED AND HILARIOUS FRIEND
PIERRE-YVES "HAMO". – J.D.

First published 2023 by Walker Books Ltd
87 Vauxhall Walk, London SE11 5HJ

2 4 6 8 10 9 7 5 3 1

Text © 2023 Mewrite Ltd
Illustrations © 2023 Joëlle Dreidemy

The right of Larry Hayes and Joëlle Dreidemy to be identified as author and illustrator
respectively of this work has been asserted in accordance with the
Copyright, Designs and Patents Act 1988

This book has been typeset in Futura, Academy Engraved, Annie Use Your Telescope,
Autumn Voyage, Display Patrol, Fat Free Solid, Likely, Liquid Embrace, Malayalam
Sangam, Marker Monkey, Minion, Ribeye, Travelling Typewriter and Wingdings

Printed and bound by CPI Group (UK) Ltd, Croydon, CR0 4YY

British Library Cataloguing in Publication Data:
a catalogue record for this book is available from the British Library

ISBN 978-1-5295-0663-1

www.walker.co.uk

All activities are for information and/or entertainment purposes only.
Adult supervision is required for all activities.

WALKER
BOOKS

FSC
www.fsc.org
MIX
Paper | Supporting
responsible forestry
FSC® C171272

HOW TO BE A
KID
BOSS

LARRY HAYES

ILLUSTRATED BY JOËLLE DREIDEMY

⚡✦✱ CONTENTS ⊙✱⊙

HOW TO GET JEDI MIND POWERS

EVERYBODY KNOWS:

Jedi only exist in movies and no one can really move things with mind powers, or blast lightning out of their hands, or control the weak-minded. No one can really do any of that *Star Wars* stuff. It's just special effects.

BUT SECRET 1 IS THIS:

George Lucas, who created *Star Wars*, based the Jedi and their powers on Tibetan monks. He'd heard reports that monks were practising Abhijñ (you pronounce it, "Uh-bee-janar"), a set of techniques that let them do everything from flying to mind control.

After the first *Star Wars* movie, a team from Harvard Medical School travelled to Tibet to investigate these powers. The good news is that those Harvard scientists described the meditation technique in full. If you want Jedi mind powers, there are two ways you can go.

METHOD 1: Study and practise the ancient art of Abhijñ. Many religious centres, located deep within the Himalayas, keep these powerful meditative procedures a closely guarded secret. But if you want to see if you do have any natural ability, why not start small? Try the meditative super-hot finger technique.

METHOD 2: Cheat. If you want to cheat, the best place to start is secret 72: How to get Jedi mind powers (cheat method).

PUT IT TO THE TEST:

HOW TO GET A
SUPER–HOT FINGER:

4. Breathe in through your nose, out through your mouth. Focus on your breath and go slow – aim for four seconds to breathe in, four to breathe out.

3. Empty your mind! Thoughts will pop up, but just let them drift away.

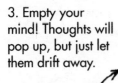

2. Close your eyes.

1. Sit comfortably.

5. Place your hands on your belly. Let it relax and feel it moving in and out as you breathe.

REPEAT THE NEXT THREE STEPS OVER AND OVER.

6. In your mind, picture having an empty body.

8. With every breath, imagine the lamp getting hotter and hotter.

7. Imagine your finger is a hot lamp.

IMPORTANT: You'll need to practise every day. Start with five minutes and work your way up to 30 minutes. Once you've been practising for a while, test your finger. Measure your finger temperature before and after your practice. For a practical application of this Jedi mind power, see secret 63: How to get rid of a verruca.

HOW TO TELL IF SOMEONE'S LYING

EVERYBODY KNOWS:

It's impossible to tell if someone's lying. If people could, then there would be no crime, no crime movies, no fun and teenagers would always be grounded. There are a million reasons why lying was invented, and human civilization wouldn't last five minutes if nobody could lie. In fact, scientific studies have shown that about a third of the population lies every single day.

WHY LYING WAS INVENTED

BUT SECRET 2 IS THIS:

You can tell if someone's lying if you know what to look out for. But most people get it wrong because they have incorrect ideas about what liars do when they lie.

HOW TO GET IT WRONG (SUCKER):

MYTH 1:
"LIARS LOOK TO THE LEFT"
WRONG!

MYTH 2:
"LIARS SCRATCH THEIR NOSE"
WRONG!

MYTH 3:
"LIARS BLUSH"
WRONG!

MYTH 4:
"LIARS SWALLOW BEFORE THEY SPEAK"
GLOUPS
WRONG!

PUT IT TO THE TEST:

There's no single clue that tells you if someone is lying. For example, liars do often scratch their noses, but so do people with itchy noses.

But don't worry, you can still spot a liar if you know how, and the secret is simple. When most people tell the truth their face, voice, body and words all communicate the same thing. But when most people lie their face, voice, body and words DON'T MATCH UP.

HEAD IS AT A JAUNTY ANGLE

BOOM

MOUTH IS HALF-SMILING

VOICE IS HIGH PITCHED

A LABELLED LIAR

But the best way to tell if things aren't matching up is to just go with your gut feeling. If something sounds off, then it probably is. If you're not sure you can nail this one, remember: practice makes perfect. And practice is child's play, literally. Just play two truths and a lie.

HOW TO PLAY TWO TRUTHS AND A LIE:

Sit in a circle with some friends or family members. Each person shares three things about themselves. Two are true, one is a lie. You have to guess which is the lie. Play this game with enough people and you'll become a human lie detector. Just tune in to what you feel and follow your gut instinct (or cheat). If you turn out to be weirdly good at this game – you might make a brilliant secret agent. Check out secret 83: How to become a secret agent.

CHEAT CODE:
SHUT YOUR EYES.
What you see is probably just distracting you so shut your eyes and listen. You'll immediately be a better lie detector.

SECRET NUMBER ③

HOW TO TRAIN YOUR PARENTS (LIKE A PERFORMING SEAL)

EVERYBODY KNOWS:
Grown-ups think they're in charge, and they won't be told what to do – especially by their own kids. Parents will always do what they want and there's nothing you can do about it.

BUT SECRET 3 IS THIS:
Parents are humans, just like us. And like animals, they can be trained. Your best bet is to use the same techniques used by seal trainers. These techniques are so powerful that people have used them to teach a chicken how to win a game of noughts and crosses.

If animal trainers can get a baboon to do this:

Then we're sure you can get your parent to do this:

HERE'S THE TRICK:
Animal trainers reward behaviour that they like. But that's only half of it. The BIG LESSON from animal trainers is to totally ignore behaviour you don't like. The idea is that any response to a behaviour encourages it. So when a seal does something wrong, the trainer just stands very still, careful not to look at the seal, and then goes back to work. The idea is that if a behaviour provokes no response then it fades away.

PUT IT TO THE TEST:

1. CHOOSE YOUR GOAL
Some things are never going to work. But there is a lot you can do. Maybe you want more screen time or sweets. Or maybe you're called Poppy, but your dad still calls you "Poopy" and you want him to stop.

2. CHOOSE YOUR REWARD
With a baboon, a banana works. A seal? Raw fish. With a parent, you're more likely to succeed if you reward them with praise.

3. IGNORE THEM
When they get it wrong, ignore them completely. If your dad calls you Poopy, don't get annoyed, don't complain, just say nothing.

4. BIG PRAISE!
When they get it right, give them praise, thanks and attention. Soon, "Poopy" will be a thing of the past...

HOW TO GET AWAY WITH THE WORLD'S FUNNIEST PRACTICAL JOKE

EVERYBODY KNOWS:

Practical jokes are both funny and annoying. And the funnier they are the more annoying they get. So you will always get in big trouble for a really good practical joke. And the world's funniest practical joke will get you into the world's biggest trouble.

BUT SECRET 4 IS THIS:

You can get away with the world's funniest practical joke – it just takes a bit of planning. First you need to know the trick. It's called "Cling film on the toilet and hope they don't poop".

PUT IT TO THE TEST:

Doing this practical joke is easy: get some cling film, lift up the toilet seat and stretch the cling film across the toilet bowl. Make sure you stretch it tightly and evenly, so it can't be seen. Then wait until someone needs the toilet and hope they only do a wee.

If you're worried about being told off for this harmless practical joke, remember the following:

1. Tell your victim that wee is cleaner than tap water! (Yes, there are fewer bacteria in urine!)
2. Show you're actually a responsible human being by doing any mopping-up required.
3. Remind your victim that writer Mark Twain famously said, "Humour is mankind's greatest blessing."
4. Apologize. A lot.
5. Don't call them "wee bum" for at least a week.

HOW TO MAKE SOMEONE THINK THEY'VE GOT A BIG RUBBER HAND

EVERYBODY KNOWS:

People don't usually have a big rubber hand. But think again!

BUT SECRET 5 IS THIS:

You can completely freak someone out by making someone think they've got a big rubber hand. All you need is 60 seconds, a rubber washing-up glove, a big piece of cardboard and two small paintbrushes.

PUT IT TO THE TEST:

First practise on yourself using these steps. Once you've cracked the technique, you can do it on anyone.

HELP, I'VE GOT A BIG RUBBER HAND!

1. Blow up the glove and tie a knot in it to make a rubber hand.

2. Place the rubber hand on a table in front of you. Hide your real hand behind the cardboard.

PFFF

3. Now get somebody to stroke and tap both the rubber hand and your real hand. They must make identical movements with both paintbrushes.

4. Keep looking at the fake hand until the illusion kicks in (60 seconds tops). You'll start to feel the paintbrush on your big rubber hand!

5. Try not to freak out. You can do loads of stuff with this technique – your imagination is the limit.

HOW TO BE A GHOSTBUSTER

EVERYBODY KNOWS:

Ghosts exist. In fact, most people (three out of five!) have even seen an **ACTUAL GHOST**. Millions of trustworthy people experience weird stuff happening every year, from things jumping off shelves to actual sightings of ghosts. So if you do get the chance to go somewhere famously haunted, you'd better be prepared.

BUT SECRET 6 IS THIS:

Ghosts don't really exist. Probably. OK, so it's really hard to prove something doesn't exist. There's only one real way for you to be absolutely certain. You need to become a ghostbuster. Yes, you need to go somewhere super haunted and check it out yourself. And the only way YOU will be certain is if YOU are the one to do it. If you're worried about being dragged into the netherworld, then take someone who is less lucky than you (see secret 11: How to be lucky).

ALWAYS BUST GHOSTS WITH AN UNLUCKY FRIEND.

Only two things can happen:
First, you need to understand why people think they've seen a ghost.

1. Nothing happens = great! You now know ghosts don't exist

2. Your unlucky friend gets sucked into the netherworld = great! You now know ghosts do exist

Scientists think ghost sightings are caused by three things that can make you feel **WEIRD**:

1. Sounds you don't hear
2. Magnets you don't notice
3. Air pressure you don't feel

Second, you'll need to find somewhere **SUPER HAUNTED**. This isn't difficult. There are thousands of haunted places around the world so there's bound to be one near you.

PUT IT TO THE TEST:

Science can explain away all ghosts with just four ghostbuster gadgets.

GHOSTBUSTER TOOLKIT:

COMPASS
(FOR DETECTING A
MAGNETIC FIELD)

BAROMETER
(FOR MEASURING
AIR PRESSURE)

PIGEON
(FOR DETECTING
HIDDEN SOUNDS)

TRAINERS
(FOR RUNNING AWAY)

GHOSTBUSTER GADGET 1: PIGEON

Infrasound is sound so low that you can't hear it but you can sense it. Sometimes it makes your eyeballs vibrate, so you see weird things. It also vibrates your brain and can make you feel funny. Scientists have found that loads of haunted places have infrasound. You can download a free "infrasound detector" app on to a phone. But if you don't have access to a phone, don't worry – just get a pigeon. Pigeons use infrasound to navigate. And, luckily, they are everywhere and easy to train. Basically, if your pigeon goes a bit wild then it's because it can hear infrasound.

A twitchy pigeon means ghosts are not real.

GHOSTBUSTER GADGET 2: COMPASS

Most ghosts can be explained by magnetics. When scientists investigated super-haunted Hampton Court Palace in London, they found that the rooms where people saw ghosts had one thing in common: they all had changes in the magnetic field. These magnetic changes were affecting people's brains (because brain cells use electricity and magnetic fields can create an electrical charge). To test for this, you just need a compass. Point it north and then walk round the room. Any change in the magnetic field will cause the compass to twitch.

A twitchy compass means ghosts are not real.

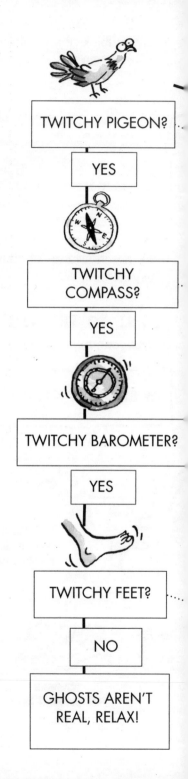

TWITCHY PIGEON?

YES

TWITCHY COMPASS?

YES

TWITCHY BAROMETER?

YES

TWITCHY FEET?

NO

GHOSTS AREN'T REAL, RELAX!

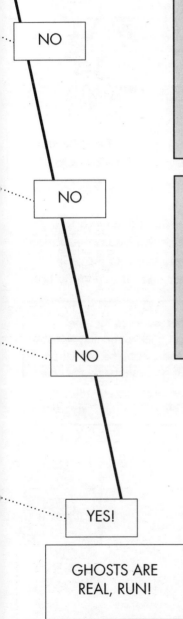

NO

NO

NO

YES!

GHOSTS ARE
REAL, RUN!

GHOSTBUSTER GADGET 3: BAROMETER

Lots of spooky events can be explained by air pressure changes. These can trigger brain cells in the bit of your brain that processes information from your senses. This causes your brain to see something weird... To test for changes in air pressure, borrow a barometer – they are old-fashioned tools for predicting the weather by measuring air pressure.

A twitchy barometer means ghosts are not real.

GHOSTBUSTER GADGET 4: TRAINERS

If gadgets 1, 2 and 3 are not twitchy but your feet are twitchy, then it's probably best to do a runner before you get sucked into the netherworld.

If the only thing twitching is your feet then ghosts are real! Run!

HOW TO SURVIVE IN A DESERT

EVERYBODY KNOWS:

Nobody survives for long stranded in the desert.
Humans die of thirst long before they die of hunger. So if you get stuck in a desert, you'll probably be vulture food by the end of the first day.

BUT SECRET 7 IS THIS:

If you're unlucky enough to get lost in a desert, you can survive.
Thousands of species have made a home in the desert and not just plants and nocturnal animals, humans too. Many people live and thrive in deserts. And you too can survive in the desert for ages if you know how.

> **FUN FACT:** Lost marathon runner Mauro Prosperi survived for nine whole days and walked a whopping 299km to get back to running water. Prosperi was running in an infamous desert ultramarathon, the Marathon des Sables, when he got lost. OK, so he wasn't in great shape by the time he was rescued. He needed to be injected with 16 bags of liquid and he couldn't eat solids for five months. BUT he survived.

PUT IT TO THE TEST:

1. Don't eat food. Yep, you can survive for ages without food and eating will just use up body fluid. The only exception is fruit – if you can find a fruiting cactus, you're in luck. You've probably given yourself an extra few days of life. If you do eat and need the toilet, see secret 8: How to wipe your bum in a desert.

2. Don't drink water. Take a sip and then hold it in your mouth. Only drink when your wee is dark yellow.

3. Keep your cool. Most people panic. Most people die. So stay calm, and stay put. Let rescuers find you.

4. Keep your mouth shut. It can slow down dehydration by 25 per cent. Cover your face with a cloth bandana to slow it even more.

5. Get a hat. If you don't have one, make one using your pants.

6. Get cosy. When the sun goes down, it'll get cold very quickly. Keep those pants on your head and try to stay warm. Get snug by a rock or pile up some sand to provide protection against the wind.

7. Make your mark. Help rescuers find you by making a mark in the desert. When the sun is low and cooler, use that time to make a giant cross out of stones.

HOW TO WIPE YOUR BUM IN A DESERT

EVERYBODY KNOWS:

Deserts are famous for sand and cactuses. So don't wipe your bum in the desert. Wait until you get back.

HOW TO SEE A FLYING PIG (CHEAT METHOD)

EVERYBODY KNOWS:
Pigs can't fly. There's even a famous saying about it.

BUT SECRET 9 IS THIS:
There's always a way. Even if it's a cheaty way.

PUT IT TO THE TEST:

1. First, draw the pig's head to the left of the landscape page.

2. Next, draw the pig's body.

3. Finally, draw the pig's tail.

4. To transform your pig into a bird, flip your drawing so it is portrait. You can try drawing different animals with this optical illusion too.

HOW TO WIN ROCK, PAPER, SCISSORS

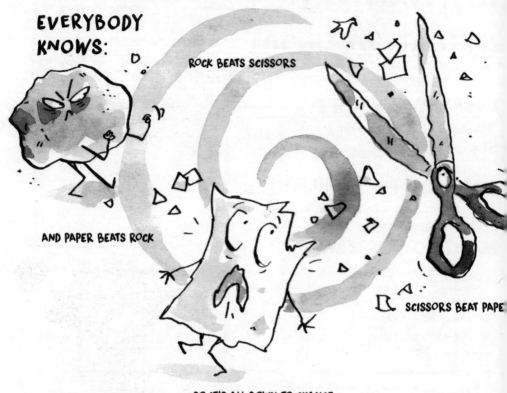

EVERYBODY KNOWS:

ROCK BEATS SCISSORS

AND PAPER BEATS ROCK

SCISSORS BEAT PAPE

SO IT'S ALL DOWN TO CHANCE

BUT SECRET 10 IS THIS:

Scientific research shows there is a way to win. You just need to understand two secrets about how brains work…

BRAIN SECRET 1: People go with rock the most – because it feels strong and powerful.

BRAIN SECRET 2: If people win, they usually stick with the same thing. If they lose, they switch.

You can exploit these two secrets to win most of the time…

PUT IT TO THE TEST:

1. Start with paper (because the other person is most likely to start with rock).

2. If you WIN, switch to what the other person just did (because they will likely switch).

ROUND 1.
YOU DO ... PAPER
THEY DO ... ROCK

ROUND 2.
SWITCH TO ROCK!

3. If you LOSE, switch to what they didn't do (because they will stick).

ROUND 1. YOU DO ... PAPER
THEY DO ... SCISSORS

ROUND 2.
SWITCH TO ROCK!

4. If in doubt, go with paper.

You can now beat anyone, most of the time, at rock, paper, scissors. Remember: knowledge is POWER. Power to do fewer chores, get free sweets, take over the world...

ROCK, PAPER, SCISSORS TO SEE IF I GO TO SCHOOL THIS WEEK

WARNING! After a while, your family will avoid having rock, paper, scissors battles with you. You need a new plan ... see secret 56: How to win a coin toss.

HOW TO BE LUCKY

HI!!

EVERYBODY KNOWS:

You're either lucky or you're not. That's what lucky means, right? It's all down to chance. And all that superstitious touching-wood, four-leaf-clover, rabbit's-foot stuff? It's rubbish. We only do it because we're desperate. If a rabbit's foot really brought good luck, then the rabbit would still have a foot.

BUT SECRET 11 IS THIS:

You can change your luck. Scientists have studied the whole "luck thing" and one scientist – a guy called Professor Richard Wiseman – even set up a Luck School where you can learn to be lucky. Prof Wiseman found four things that can change your luck.

PUT IT TO THE TEST:

LESSON 1: TRY STUFF

People who are open to new experiences create, notice and act upon the chance opportunities in their life. And research shows that the old saying is true: "You most regret the things you didn't do." So get out there and just try more stuff.

LESSON 2: LISTEN TO HUNCHES

Your unconscious brain is brilliant at seeing patterns that your conscious brain hasn't even noticed. So when in doubt, go with your gut – 90 per cent of lucky people trust their feelings and instincts when it comes to making decisions.

FUN FACT: Your conscious brain is the stuff you're aware of thinking. But your brain is full of other unconscious thoughts too – thoughts that you're not aware of. For example, your unconscious brain tells your body to breathe and blink and keep your bum shut.

LESSON 3: EXPECT GOOD LUCK

Be optimistic! Luck School showed that people who expect things to work out well have more GRIT – they kept going when other people gave up. What's more, science has shown that lucky charms actually do work, but only if you believe in it. Lucky charms can boost people's self-confidence and that improves their performance. For example, even just wishing someone good luck before a sports match can help them play better.

LESSON 4: TURN BAD LUCK INTO GOOD

But surely a bit of positive thinking and a lucky charm can't save you, right? Wrong. The secret is to find a silver lining in every dark cloud. The more you think like this the quicker your luck will turn around. Remember: your brain is constantly changing. And you can change your brain just by focusing on different things. So if you start looking for positives and examples of good luck, then you'll keep noticing more and more in the future.

WARNING! No amount of positive thinking will help you win a fight with a tiger. For that, you have to cheat – see secret 15: How to fight a tiger (and win).

HOW TO BUILD A SUPER MEMORY

EVERYBODY KNOWS:

Some people are naturally good at remembering stuff – but the rest of us are not. We forget when to bring in our PE kit, and what a "fronted adverbial" is, and what "parallel" means and how to spell "desparate"*
... hold on, what were we talking about?

BUT SECRET 12 IS THIS:

The man with the world's best memory used to have a really bad memory. Eight-times World Memory Champion Dominic O'Brien really struggled to remember stuff when he was a kid until he stumbled across the secret to building a super memory. There's nothing special about O'Brien's memory, he claims. The secret is all in having a memory palace – a memory technique so powerful that it could turn you into a real-life Sherlock Holmes: able to pass every exam, learn any language and never forget anything.

PUT IT TO THE TEST:

1. CHOOSE YOUR PALACE

Using your own home is easiest. Imagine walking through your home step by step, and work out a number of places where you could imagine "things". Write down the places in the right order.

For example, you might start with a front porch, then a coat rack,

and then a shoe cupboard and so on... Aim for ten.

* Editor's note: He means "desperate".

2. WALK THROUGH

Walk through your home in the right order and spend five seconds staring at each of your ten places. Then do it again – but this time with just your imagination. Keep repeating until you're confident you can do the same every time.
You're now ready to remember ten things!

3. MAKE A "MEMORY PEG"

Make up a weird visual image for each thing you want to remember – it's called a "memory peg" because it's something to hook your memory on to. The only rule here is the weirder the image the better. Let's say it's for a French test and the first word is "hedgehog". In French, this is "hérisson", which sounds a bit like "hairy son". Now, all you have to do is imagine a werewolf version of a little boy, holding a hedgehog.

4. PUT THE MEMORY PEG IN PLACE

Put each image in one of your "places" in the order that you remember them. So start with the front porch...

Once you've set up your memory palace, you can reuse it to remember anything you like. And best of all, as long as you use it every now and again, it can keep working for the rest of your life. Not everyone can develop a super memory. We all have different brains that are good at some things and worse at others. But however good or bad your memory – then a memory palace is likely to make it better.

HOW TO MAKE SOMEBODY DRIBBLE

EVERYBODY KNOWS:

The only way to make somebody dribble is to tie them up and not feed them for a day, and then wave a bacon sandwich in front of them. And everybody knows that you can get arrested and sent to jail for that sort of thing.

BUT SECRET 13 IS THIS:

There's an easier way to make somebody dribble. It takes hardly any effort and is really quick and easy.

WITH A FEW SIMPLE STEPS YOU CAN TURN AN OLDER SIBLING FROM THIS ...

INTO THIS!

FUN FACT: A guy called Ivan Pavlov discovered that if he rang a bell every time a dog was given food, then after a while he could make the dog dribble just by ringing the bell. We're not sure why he did this. And we're not sure why you'd want to do this to your family. But if you do, here's how.

PUT IT TO THE TEST:

All you need is a small handbell. And some victims, like your family.

BELL

METHOD: Every time you sit down to eat, just before your victims are about to put the first forkful of food in their gobs … ring the bell. If anyone asks what you're doing, explain that it's a science project. After about two weeks of doing this (at every meal), your subjects should be ready.

Now, whenever you want them to start dribbling, just ring the bell. If you need to stop your family dribbling, please check out book two. Coming to all good bookshops soon(ish).

VICTIMS

WARNING!
This will also work on you. So wear ear defenders if you don't want to start dribbling every time you hear a bell.

HOW TO GET SWEETS FOR BREAKFAST

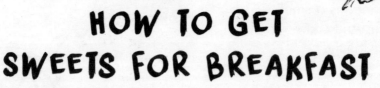

EVERYBODY KNOWS:

No parent would let their kids eat sweets for breakfast. There's a good reason for that: they are programmed to worry about you. And above all, they worry about your health. Worse still, they don't trust you to be sensible about your own sugar intake. That's because they still think of you as a clueless four year old who would eat three scoops of ice cream and then be sick – even though you only did that the one time.

BUT SECRET 14 IS THIS:

Getting sweets for breakfast is child's play. You need to persuade your parents that eating sweets for breakfast is actually a sign that you're going to grow up to be super healthy and super successful as a grown-up. To do this, you need to teach them one killer secret: being able to wait is a key to success and good health in life.

YOU NEED TO CHANGE WHAT YOUR PARENTS THINK.

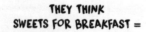

THEY THINK SWEETS FOR BREAKFAST =

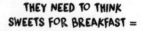

THEY NEED TO THINK SWEETS FOR BREAKFAST =

PUT IT TO THE TEST:

1. REASSURE THE GROWN-UP

Ask them to buy a pack of sweets for "an experiment". Then tell them to leave you in a room with five sweets. The rule is: if you can avoid eating the sweets for half an hour, you'll get ten sweets. Tell them that if you pass this test, then scientists have shown that you are much more likely to be successful and healthy as a grown-up.

2. TAKE THE TEST

WARNING! DO NOT EAT THE SWEETS!

FAIL!

3. WHEN THE 30 MINUTES ARE UP, DO NOT EAT THE TEN SWEETS!

Unbelievable right!? You've earned ten sweets and you're not going to eat them? It's like you're a super-advanced cyborg with willpower the size of a planet.

SUCCESS!

4. TAKE IT TO THE NEXT LEVEL

Shock your parents by telling them that you're going to resist the ten sweets all night. And if you do, you'll get twelve sweets at breakfast time. Their brain will explode.

Now set your alarm, and when it rings ... eat those sweets!

CHEAT CODE: If your parents still need persuading, tell them this killer fact: twelve gummy bears have the same sugar as two bowls of cereal. Offer to have porridge or eggs for breakfast for three days, instead of cereal, to balance things out.

HOW TO FIGHT A TIGER (AND WIN)

EVERYBODY KNOWS:

You can't fight a tiger and win. They're twenty times stronger than you and twice as fast. A tiger can carry the weight of six humans in its mouth and still run up some stairs. Plus, their jaws are twice as strong as a lion's, so you won't win even if you're a lion. And if none of that puts you off, remember: their claws are like five super-sharp knives. One swipe from a paw and you're a goner.

WARNING! A tiger could kill you with three paws tied behind its back. Maybe four.

BUT SECRET 15 IS THIS:

You can fight off a tiger – and that counts as a win in our book.

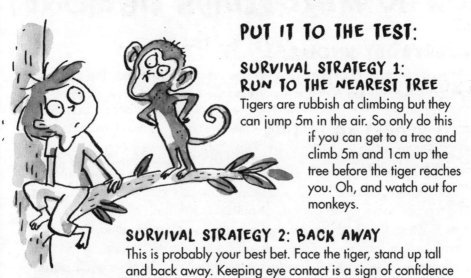

PUT IT TO THE TEST:

SURVIVAL STRATEGY 1: RUN TO THE NEAREST TREE

Tigers are rubbish at climbing but they can jump 5m in the air. So only do this if you can get to a tree and climb 5m and 1cm up the tree before the tiger reaches you. Oh, and watch out for monkeys.

SURVIVAL STRATEGY 2: BACK AWAY

This is probably your best bet. Face the tiger, stand up tall and back away. Keeping eye contact is a sign of confidence and may give the tiger reason to hesitate. Don't stop until you're very far away. If the tiger starts to charge, scream and shout as loudly and weirdly as you can – anything to make the tiger think twice.

SURVIVAL STRATEGY 3: KARATE EYE POKE

If you get to the point where you're actually fighting a tiger, then it'll probably be the last – but most interesting – experience of your short life. Just about nothing will work.

However, the story of Gōgen Yamaguchi, a Japanese karate expert, may suggest a way. Yamaguchi was captured during the Second World War and put in a cage with a tiger as a punishment. According to his autobiography, he won. And it's thought that the old karate eye poke was his secret weapon. (But remember: the tiger's autobiography may say something completely different.)

HOW TO MAKE LOADS OF MONEY

EVERYBODY KNOWS:

When it comes to pocket money, you get what you're given. The only way to get more is to do loads of chores around the house and hope for the best.

BUT SECRET 16 IS THIS:

Forget about doing extra chores – most grown-ups don't pay anything and if they do it's peanuts. BUT you don't have to settle for peanuts – even when you're a kid. If you want to make loads of money, try this... The typical home in the UK has about £4,000 worth of unwanted stuff. Yes, that's stuff nobody wants that you could sell and split the proceeds. And by selling it – so someone else can use it – you're helping the environment, because it's one less thing that needs to be manufactured.

DO

I WANT TO LEARN HOW TO MAKE MONEY

EXPLAIN WHY

DO

IF I FIND SOME STUFF YOU DON'T WANT, CAN WE SELL IT AND SPLIT THE MONEY 50:50

EXPLAIN HOW

DO

WE COULD MAKE £2,000 EACH

YAY, I'M PROUD OF YOU!

EXPLAIN WHAT

DO NOT

YOU WON'T BELIEVE IT. I JUST SOLD YOUR CAR FOR £4,000!

PUT IT TO THE TEST:

1.CHECK "HOW MUCH CAN I GET FOR IT?"

First, ask a grown-up what they want to declutter and tell them how much they could earn for each item. And remember to check out their old vintage clothes – there could be some real gems in there. Then, use a resale site to see roughly how much you'll get for different things around the house.

2. WORK WITH A PARENT TO START SELLING

Make sure you use the right resale site for your item. There are dozens of specialist resale sites that might earn you more. If you're selling vintage clothes, or antiques, or art, or big heavy items like furniture it's worth checking out different sites. Start small and build up. And make sure a grown-up does all the messaging and arranges for any pick-ups.

3. CREATE YOUR LISTING

Take photos of your item. Make sure you have a clear, clean background and good lighting with no shadows. The description is important too – see how other people have described the same item and copy what you can.

4. SCHEDULE YOUR SALE

Schedule all your sales to end on a Sunday evening to max your money. Make sure you sell things in the right season – sunglasses and bikes in spring, coats in the autumn, Halloween stuff in October, and so on.

HOW TO UNDERSTAND DOG

EVERYBODY KNOWS:
Dogs don't speak English.

BUT SECRET 17 IS THIS:
Modern science is unlocking the secrets of what's going on in your dog's head. And scientists have discovered that your dog is trying to talk to you using 19 different gestures. So with a bit of up-to-the-minute science, you can understand what your dog is trying to say.

> **FUN FACT:** Humans and dogs have evolved together over thousands of years and so we've learned to understand each other. Dogs may not be able to speak but they can understand what you say. A dog is able to learn around 165 words on average.

PUT IT TO THE TEST:
Dogs use 19 different gestures to communicate. But remember: different dogs will use different gestures to mean different things. So you need to watch your dog carefully and learn what they're trying to say. There is a short cut, though. Because most of the time, dogs are trying to say one of just four things.

HEAD TURN = WANT FOOD/WATER

**PAW TOUCH
= WANT TOY/PLAY**

**HEAD TURN
= WANT OUT**

**LICKING
= SCRATCH ME**

So the next time
you see a dog
do something
strange, check
out what it's
trying to say.

**SLURP,
SLURP**

HOW TO PASS A WITCH TRIAL

EVERYBODY KNOWS:

You can't pass a witch trial. The only way to prove your innocence is if you drown.

If you invent a time machine and you end up back in the 16th century, you'll probably be arrested for being a witch or warlock. Back in the 1500s, about 500 people were killed for witchcraft every year. Just wearing trainers back in the olden days would be a sure sign that you're a devil worshipper. So, best to have a plan worked out just in case.

BUT SECRET 18 IS THIS:

Luckily, that's not something we need to worry about now, because no one's been burned as a witch for ages. You should worry about being accused of other stuff instead, such as cheating on a spelling test.

PUT IT TO THE TEST:

Even now in the 21st century, people accuse others of all sorts of stuff. If that does ever happen to you, don't panic, just follow these simple, super-practical steps.

WHAT TO DO IF YOU'RE ACCUSED OF A CRIME YOU DIDN'T COMMIT:

1. DON'T GET ANGRY

If you get angry, most people will think you're guilty and trying to cover it up. So take a deep breath and try to smile before you say anything.

2. BE CONFIDENT

Remember: over half of all people tried for witchcraft were found innocent! If you show a willingness to cooperate and get to the bottom of things, you'll automatically look innocent.

3. GET JUSTICE

Whoever is deciding your guilt, ask them how you can prove your innocence. This will get them to put themselves in your shoes. Let's say you've been accused of cheating on a test. How could you prove you're innocent? Get the teacher to retest you.

But what about the whole witchcraft thing? If nothing works and you're headed for the bonfire, then you need to cheat (only use this as a last resort).

CHEAT CODE:

Admit you're a witch but explain that you were put under a spell by someone else. Then point at someone who looks more like a witch/warlock than you.

HOW TO MAKE YOUR WHOOPEE CUSHION SMELL LIKE A REAL FART

EVERYBODY KNOWS:
The only thing funnier than a whoopee cushion is putting cling film over the toilet.

BUT SECRET NUMBER 19 IS:
You can make whoopee cushions even more realistic/gross/funny by making them smell like a real fart.

WHOOPEE CUSHION

THE CAULIFLOWER TRICK:

4 DAYS LATER...

WARNING!
Your whoopee cushion will now be a bit disgusting. If you are just too sad to say goodbye to it, then get a grown-up to wash it out with antibacterial soap. Explain that it was a "useful science project" and ask them if they know how many zeros there are in 105 vigintillion.

PUT IT TO THE TEST:

1. Get some cooked cauliflower and stuff it inside your whoopee cushion. You don't need much – just a pea-sized amount.

2. Blow up the cushion and then leave it somewhere warm for about three days. Bacteria grow best at room temperature or above. If you used enough cauliflower – after three days that would get to about 105 vigintillion bacteria – which is why you only use a small amount of veg. Remember: every single bacterium will be belching out sulphur – the gas in killer farts.

CHEAT CODE:

If you don't have time to brew your cauliflower for four days, you can always try to fart into a whoopee cushion. But it's not recommended (or dignified).

PFFFF!

43

HOW TO PICK YOUR NOSE WITHOUT ANYONE NOTICING

EVERYBODY KNOWS:

Picking your nose and eating it is a disgusting habit that spreads disease. And if you make a habit of it, you will probably end up being shunned by friends and family and have to live on an island all alone.

BUT SECRET 20 IS THIS:

Bogeys taste nice for a reason. Humans have evolved to eat bogeys through natural selection.

NATURAL SELECTION AND BOGEY-EATING:

1. In the Stone Age, only some people had the gene for bogey-eating. Their immune systems grew strong because their noses and stomachs were exposed to all sorts of bacteria.

2. So when the plague came, the bogey-eaters survived.

3. These bogey-eaters had children with the same bogey-eating gene.

Today (just about) everyone in the world has the gene for bogey-eating! Unfortunately, we live in an ignorant age where bogey-eating is frowned upon. Now it's all very well being clever enough to know that eating bogeys is good for you. But you also need to be wise enough to know that you should still avoid getting caught. Basically, bogey-eating is fine as long as you follow the two golden rules.

PUT IT TO THE TEST:

GOLDEN RULE 1: DON'T GET CAUGHT

Do it in your bedroom. Or, if you have to do it somewhere else, loosen up your bogeys first by rubbing and pinching your nose on the outside. That way, you'll spend minimal time with a finger actually up your nose.

HOW TO LOOSEN UP A BOGEY:

GOLDEN RULE 2: KNOW YOUR FACTS

Even following the tips above, at some point you will get caught by a grown-up with nothing better to do than catch you picking your nose. If the grown-up shouts, "Get your fingers out of your nose!" then it's time to go on the offensive with your bogey super facts.

BOGEY SUPER FACTS

SUPER FACT 1: 91 per cent of grown-ups pick their nose (the other 9 per cent are probably lying about it).

SUPER FACT 2: Eating bogeys is good for your teeth. Yes, bogeys contain something called "salivary mucin", which stops bacteria sticking to your teeth.

SUPER FACT 3: Eating bogeys is probably good for your immune system. It may even help protect you from asthma.

CHEAT CODE:

If the grown-up still isn't convinced, try a joke:
Q. What's the difference between bogeys and broccoli?
A. Kids don't eat broccoli.

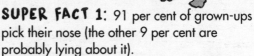

AND IF THAT DOESN'T WORK, JUST SAY, "SNOT MY FAULT, I CAN'T HELP IT."

HOW TO SURVIVE WITHOUT GROWN-UPS

EVERYBODY KNOWS:

From the minute kids are born, grown-ups treat them like royalty. They feed them, they wash them, they even wipe their bums. Living without grown-ups would be impossible and kids would die from one or all of the following:

1. Too much screen time
2. Not going to bed on time
3. Eating sweets for breakfast (see secret 14: How to get sweets for breakfast)

BUT SECRET 21 IS THIS:

Grown-ups spend their lives complaining about all the stuff they have to do, but most of it doesn't actually need doing. Do you think we're joking? Next time your parents moan about something they have to do, use the FIVE WHYS. Sakichi Toyoda, the founder of Toyota Industries, developed the FIVE WHYS technique in the 1930s and Toyota still uses it to solve problems today.

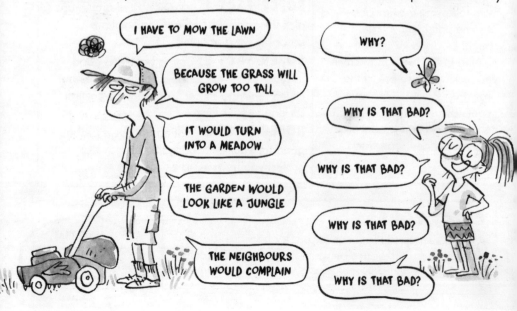

PUT IT TO THE TEST:

NO GROWN-UPS ACTION PLAN:

WHERE WILL WE GET MONEY FROM?
See secret 101: How to be a kid millionaire.

WHO WILL BUY FOOD?
Do it online and tick the "same every week" box.

WHO WILL COOK EVERY DAY?
Get take-aways and eat raw food (not raw meat, though).

WHO WILL FEED THE DOG?
Let them lick your plate clean and eat stuff that drops on the floor.

WHO DOES THE LAUNDRY?
Wear the same clothes all week (only grown-ups smell).

WHO WILL DO THE IRONING?
Don't do the ironing.

REMEMBER: The only thing that parents do that's important is playing with you.

HOW TO THROW AN EGG SO IT DOESN'T BREAK

EVERYBODY KNOWS:
Eggs break when you throw them.

BUT SECRET 22 IS THIS:
An egg won't break if you throw it high enough and it lands on grass. Eggs are incredibly strong if you apply a force at the top or bottom. In fact an Asian elephant calf, weighing about 90kg, could stand on a chicken egg and it wouldn't break.

We didn't believe it either, so we tested it in our Secrets Laboratory.
The first egg completely disappeared and was (weirdly) never seen again.
The second egg landed and IT DIDN'T BREAK.

PUT IT TO THE TEST:

1. Get an uncooked egg.

2. Find a house with an empty lawn on one side.

3. Throw the egg over the house.

4. Eat scrambled egg.

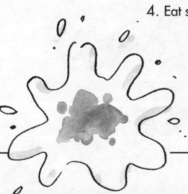

WARNING! Make sure there's no one on the other side of the house. A flying egg can badly injure someone. If you're just throwing the egg up in the air above your head then wear a helmet.

HOW TO ESCAPE FROM A ZOO

EVERYBODY KNOWS:

Hopefully you NEVER accidentally fall into an animal enclosure in a zoo. If the animals can't escape, then you don't have a hope. And the animals will probably eat you before the zookeepers save you. Even the cute ones, like meerkats and koalas and penguins, are actually savage, wild animals.

WHAT A PAIN IN THE NECK!

BUT SECRET 23 IS THIS:

It can be deathly dangerous going into an animal enclosure at a zoo and you should never do it without permission. BUT if for some strange reason you find yourself locked up in a zoo, DON'T PANIC. Zoo enclosures are animal-specific, so you just need to work out what that specific animal can't do. For example, giraffes don't have opposable thumbs so if you fall into the giraffe bit of the zoo, don't sweat it. Just use the door.

PUT IT TO THE TEST:

OK, so you're not panicking. Well done. These laws of the jungle will help with just about any animal.

LAW OF THE JUNGLE 1: DON'T RUN AWAY

Not from a carnivore, anyway – that will just trigger its hunting instinct. Back away steadily.

LAW OF THE JUNGLE 2: REMEMBER EYE CONTACT

Sometimes it's good (lions, tigers and hippos will see it as a sign of confidence and be more nervous of you); sometimes it's bad (with dogs and leopards eye contact is a sign of aggression).

LAW OF THE JUNGLE 3: MAKE FUNNY NOISES

Humans can make a massive range of noises. If all else fails, sounding like a bike horn or an opera singer might just scare a wild animal.

LAW OF THE JUNGLE 4: SWOT UP

You need to do a SWOT analysis for the specific animal enclosure you're trapped in. SWOT = Strength, Weaknesses, Opportunities and Threats. Every animal has its strengths and weaknesses. And if you're trapped in a zoo, each and every animal enclosure will have its specific opportunities and threats. If you figure those out, the battle's half won. For example, let's look at the infamous slow loris.

STRENGTHS = EXTREMELY CUTE

WEAKNESSES = EXTREMELY SLOW

S W O T

OPPORTUNITIES = YOU CAN EASILY RUN AWAY

THREATS = IT HAS POISONOUS SPIT – DON'T GET LICKED!

HOW TO ESCAPE FROM A HIPPO

THREE TIMES LONGER THAN YOU

AAAGH!

THREE TIMES FASTER THAN YOU

WEIGHS AS MUCH AS THREE SMALL CARS

A BITE THREE TIMES AS POWERFUL AS A LION'S

THE BAD NEWS:

Hippos are massive, fast and powerful. They can charge humans (and trample people when they're in a rush to get to bed).

THE GOOD NEWS:

Hippos can't climb, or stop, or change direction once they're up to speed. Hippos will only attack you if they feel threatened. And they yawn before they attack, so you should have about three seconds' warning.

JUST TELL ME THE ANSWER!

Back away, make yourself small and climb a tree or rock. If there's nothing to climb, jump to the side at the last moment.

ALSO WORKS FOR: Rhinos, buffaloes and crocodiles.

HOW TO ESCAPE FROM A MEERKAT

THE BAD NEWS:
Meerkats work well as a team and have a vicious bite. They often go for the nose.

THE GOOD NEWS:
They're smaller than you and they only attack if they feel threatened.

JUST TELL ME THE ANSWER!
Cover your nose with one hand, make yourself look small and back away. Pretending to be dead isn't a totally bad idea.

ALSO WORKS FOR: Koalas, pandas and grizzly bears.

HOW TO ESCAPE FROM A KANGAROO

THE BAD NEWS:

Kangaroos have strong back legs and sharp toenails. And they have one main fighting move: grab and kick. That toenail is like being stabbed with a knife.

WE THINK OF KANGAROOS LIKE THIS:

BUT IN REAL LIFE, THEY'RE MORE LIKE THIS:

THE GOOD NEWS:

A kangaroo will usually warn you before it attacks by scratching its tummy or going on tiptoe. And better still, there's a really simple way to tell a kangaroo that you're not a threat.

JUST TELL ME THE ANSWER!

Cough. Just give a short, deep cough. Then back away, avoiding eye contact and crouching low. Some people think kangaroos are afraid of catching human diseases. But that's nonsense. A cough is actually how kangaroos tell other kangaroos that they're not looking for a fight.

ALSO WORKS FOR: Wallabies.

HOW TO ESCAPE FROM A SHARK

THE BAD NEWS:

1. Super senses – all that stuff about sharks smelling a drop of blood a mile away? Not true, they need to be 100m away – but that's still pretty awesome.
2. Teeth – sharks have up to 3,000 teeth.
3. Skin – sharks have really rough skin, it's like sandpaper. Ouchy!

Although sharks don't eat humans, they might mistake you for a seal – or they might just bite to see what you taste like.

THE GOOD NEWS

1. Weak spots – sharks have sensitive eyes, gills and noses.
2. Quite nice – only 12 species of shark (out of 375) will ever attack a human. And even then only by mistake.

JUST TELL ME THE ANSWER!

1. Check to see which shark is in the tank you've fallen into. If it's a great white, tiger, hammerhead or bull shark, you might be in trouble. Leopard shark? Not so much. It's one of the least dangerous sharks on the planet.
2. Punch the shark if it attacks you, just under the nose. That's where it has a jelly-filled sack that it uses to detect electrical fields. Punching here will usually scare the shark away. Poking a shark in the eye often works too.
3. Get away – shark tanks are designed to help humans climb out so that should be easy enough. But if you're in the ocean, swim backwards to the shore or boat. Always try to face the shark so you can be ready to spot the next attack.

ALSO WORKS FOR: Dolphins (if they ever go rogue).

HOW TO ESCAPE FROM A KING COBRA

THE BAD NEWS:

The king cobra is one of the most venomous snakes on the planet. It can "stand up" and look you in the eye (which, based on our lived experience, is pant-fill-scary).

THE GOOD NEWS:

King cobras are slower than other snakes. They have poor eyesight and rely on smell and sensing vibrations. Also, they are scared of you. And they're rubbish when it's cold because they're cold-blooded.

JUST TELL ME THE ANSWER!

Don't bother with snake charming – that takes a lot of practice. Try this technique instead.

1. Stomp your feet and shout loudly.
2. Give the snake room to run away.
3. Use a forked stick to pin its neck.

ALSO WORKS FOR: All other snakes.

GO AWAY!

HOW TO ESCAPE FROM A POISON DART FROG

THE BAD NEWS:

The poison on a poison dart frog's skin is so powerful that one drop can kill a human.

The most deadly of all is the golden poison frog. it has enough toxin in its skin to kill 20,000 mice or 20 grown-ups.

THE GOOD NEWS:

A poison dart frog is small and soft and easily squished. And it's really only interested in being left alone. As long as you don't lick it, touch it or even go near it, you should be OK.

JUST TELL ME THE ANSWER!

Better still though, just leave it alone. Lots of poison dart frogs now appear on the endangered species list because they're losing their jungle habitat. So do the world a favour and stop squishing frogs.

ALSO WORKS FOR: Poisonous toads.

HOW TO LIE
(AND GET AWAY WITH IT)

EVERYBODY KNOWS:

We've already shared secret 2: How to tell if someone's lying. So basically, you're stuffed, because everyone in the world will buy this book.

BUT SECRET 30 IS THIS:

You can fight back! There are special techniques to help you get away with lying. Because hey, everyone does it now and again – and you will, too. So you might as well do it right.

HOW NOT TO LIE:

There first thing is to find out if you're naturally good at lying. Remember: your natural ability is just your start point – not your end point. How good you get at lying is all down to you and how much you practise. Playing the two truths and a lie game (see page 11) can improve your lying ability enormously. But if you want to get good fast, we've got you covered. Scientists have studied brilliant liars to find out how they do it. And they've found five big secrets to getting away with lying.

PUT IT TO THE TEST:

1. Picture the lie – every bit of it, step by step. That way you'll be remembering your imagined events.

THE DOG REALLY DID EAT MY HOMEWORK

2. Keep eye contact – liars often look away.

3. Relax – breathing properly will help.

4. Look happy, not defensive. Act like you don't care if the person believes you or not.

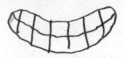

5. Control your hands – keep them away from your face.

WARNING! Excessive lying is bad for your health. It raises stress hormones. So only lie when you really need to. And never lie about something that could put you in danger.

HOW TO DISCOVER YOUR HIDDEN SUPERPOWER

EVERYBODY KNOWS:

To gain a superpower, you have to be bitten by something radioactive, be a genetic mutant, come from a different planet, or be a billionaire who can invent loads of cool stuff. And even then, you still have to choose the right costume, get a deadly enemy and sign a movie deal.

HOW TO BECOME A SUPERHERO:

OUCH!

RADIOACTIVE SPIDER

BUT SECRET 31 IS THIS:

That's rubbish. We all have hidden superpowers – we just have to discover them and then super boost them with training.

PUT IT TO THE TEST:

TEST 1: ARE YOU A SUPER LEADER?

Can you think clearly even when the stakes are high and the pressure is on?

TAKE THE PRESSURE TEST:

Get some sweets, a dice and a friend or family member. Roll the dice 17 times. Add up your score and divide it by your age. Did you get a number more or less than six? If you guessed the answer right, you get the sweets. If not, your friend gets them. Talk about pressure.

> SO, DID YOU GET THE SWEETS?
> YES = YOU CAN MAKE HIGH-RISK, HIGH-PRESSURE DECISIONS – YOU ARE A BORN LEADER (OR YOU MIGHT JUST BE LUCKY, WHICH IS GOOD TOO)
> NO = NOT TO WORRY, ANYONE CAN LEARN TO BE A SUPER LEADER. GO TO SECRET 66: HOW TO BE A LEADER

> MORE THAN 7CM = AVERAGE
> 4–7CM = YOU COULD HAVE A SUPERPOWER
> LESS THAN 4CM = BETTER THAN SPIDERMAN

TEST 2: DO YOU HAVE SUPER REACTIONS?

Do you have the reactions of a champion gamer?

TAKE THE RULER TEST:

Get a ruler and ask a friend to hold it at the top, with their arm stretched out. Put your thumb and index finger slightly open at the bottom of the ruler, with the ruler between your fingers. When your friend lets go, stop the ruler with your fingers as quickly as you can. Record how many centimetres it dropped before you stopped it. However well or badly you did, you can always train your reactions to be faster. Go to secret 42: How to get super reactions.

TEST 3: ARE YOU A SUPER ATHLETE?

Do you have fast muscles? Muscle fibres come in two types too – "fast twitch" and "slow twitch". If you have lots of "fast twitch" you'll be better at sprinting. And if you have "slow twitch" then long distance might be for you. These two tests are for runners and will show whether you're naturally better at sprinting or long distance.

TAKE THE JUMP TEST:

1. See how high you can reach. Stand next to a wall with your feet flat on the floor, reach as high as you can and make a chalk mark. Measure the height with a tape measure.
2. See how high you can jump. Warm up your muscles and jump as high as you can from standing (no run-up) and mark the height again. Do this a total of three times.

> A SUPER ATHLETIC 10 YEAR OLD CAN JUMP ABOUT 27CM (GIRLS 26CM, BOYS 28CM). AND THAT GOES UP BY 3CM EVERY YEAR.

TAKE THE SIT TEST:

Hold a wall sit for as long you can.

BACK AGAINST THE WALL

STOMACH MUSCLES TIGHT

KNEES AT 90 DEGREES

FEET FLAT ON THE GROUND

> MORE THAN 30 SECONDS = PRETTY GOOD
> MORE THAN A MINUTE = SUPER LONG-DISTANCE RUNNER!

TEST 4: DO YOU HAVE A SUPER MEMORY?

Do you know the difference between someone with a super memory and the rest of us? Super brainiacs can remember a nine-digit phone number when we can only remember a seven-digit number. Yes, you read that right, two digits – that's the big difference between being amazing and average.

TAKE THE NUMBER TEST:

Look at the following number for five seconds, then shut the book and write it down.

375 639 0031

HOW MANY DIGITS DID YOU GET RIGHT? IF YOU GOT THEM ALL RIGHT, YOU PROBABLY HAVE A SUPER MEMORY! IT'S TIME TO TRAIN YOUR MEMORY TO THE MAX – SEE SECRET 12: HOW TO BUILD A SUPER MEMORY.

TEST 5: ARE YOU A SUPERTASTER?

This might sound like a bit of a rubbish superpower – but did you know that a professional supertaster can earn millions?!

TAKE THE TASTE TEST:

Count your taste buds. How? First, put a drop of food colouring on your tongue and they'll show up as little dots. Then take a piece of paper, make a hole in it with a hole punch (8mm wide) and place it on your tongue. Count the number of circles you can see within the hole.

THE AVERAGE PERSON HAS AROUND 20. IF YOU COUNT 50 OR MORE, YOU ARE A SUPERTASTER.

SUPER BOOST YOUR POWERS

You can still get just about any superpower you want. Practice and training will get most children most superpowers. So, whether you have natural superpowers or not, it's time to … PRACTISE. The greatest superpower of all is super persistence, the ability to never give up. So, pick your superpower and get training.

HOW TO TALK SO
GROWN-UPS WILL LISTEN

EVERYBODY KNOWS:

Grown-ups know best. You should listen to them more, and follow all their rules about scissors and stuff, and if you keep bouncing on the bed you will probably die at some point.

BUT SECRET 32 IS THIS:

Most parents and carers think their job is to tell you what to do. And so, most of them aren't actually very good at listening. Don't believe me? Try this simple test.

NEXT TIME YOUR GROWN-UP IS RUSHING AROUND, COOKING AND STUFF, SAY:

I'M GOING TO PLAY LEGO LATER. I WANT TO MAKE A REAL BOMB USING DYNAMITE AND YELLOW BRICKS

OK, DARLING

If your grown-up answers "OK!" then the chances are that they weren't listening. The thing is, though, it can be really helpful if you can get your parents to listen when you need them to.

PUT IT TO THE TEST:

It's not all down to you, but there are things you can do to help.

1. Decide on a clear goal. Do you want to eat less broccoli? More sweets? Or do you just want your grown-up to play more and nag less?

2. Time it right. Wait for a moment when they're not looking, like this:

3. Use "I" statements and avoid sentences that start with "you". When you say "I feel...", you are basically taking responsibility for your own emotions, instead of trying to "blame" them on someone else. When you use the "you" word, it can make the other person feel attacked.

DON'T SAY:
"YOU HATE ME SO MUCH, WHY DON'T YOU JUST POISON ME?"

DO SAY:
"I AM OFF BROCCOLI AT THE MOMENT. CAN WE HAVE PEAS INSTEAD?"

ACTIVE LISTENING IS EASY – JUST REPEAT BACK WHAT THEY'VE SAID.

I'M SICK AND TIRED OF PICKING YOUR COAT UP OFF THE FLOOR

I HEAR YOU, MUM ... YOU'RE SICK OF PICKING MY COAT UP OFF THE FLOOR

I'LL TRY TO DO BETTER

THANK YOU, YOU'RE THE BEST

4. If they still won't listen, you'll have to teach them. Yep, you can teach grown-ups stuff, too. But if you expect your parents to listen to you, you kind of have to listen to them too (sometimes). Active listening is a great technique that shows others you're listening to their point of view.

HOW TO GET ANY TOY IN THE WORLD

EVERYBODY KNOWS:

That you can write to Santa and beg your parents all you want but, in the end, they decide what toys you get.

TYRANNOSCOOTER WILL EAT YOUR TEACHER! ONLY £499!

MERMAID SHOES BECAUSE ONLY LOSERS CAN'T WALK ON WATER

IF YOUR PARENTS LOVE YOU, THEY WILL BUY YOU a MEGASTICK!

BUT SECRET 33 IS THIS:

You can get any toy you want. First of all, you just need to understand that the key to toy economics is advertising. And the killer thing you need to know is this: you can help companies advertise. A great way to advertise is with an advertising jingle, so if you can make one up – you're laughing. Making up an advertising jingle isn't as hard as you think. An advertising jingle is just a short poem + annoying music.

PUT IT TO THE TEST:

1. Choose the toy you really want. Write down three reasons why the toy is amazing.

2. Write down some words that rhyme with your three reasons. Then make this into a poem that starts, "The wonderful thing about…"

> The wonderful thing about
>   SCOOTER:
> 1) incredibly fast
> 2) travel back to future
> 3) so fun

3. Sing your poem and record a jingle.

4. Ask a grown-up to send your jingle to the toy company and say that they can use it in return for a free toy.

> Dear Toy Company,
> Please find attached my super scooter jing…"

5. Enjoy your reward!

CHEAT CODE: If your jingle is rubbish, don't worry! Just get a really cute toddler to sing the poem, and video it. Then send that to the toy company. Make sure you get permission first!

HOW TO INVENT SOMETHING

EVERYBODY KNOWS:

You have to be a genius to invent stuff. After all, humans spent thousands of years doing poops in a hole before Thomas Crapper invented the flushing toilet. He must be a total genius, right?

BUT SECRET 34 IS THIS:

Grown-ups have old, slow brains that don't come up with many ideas. Kids have the most creative brains on the planet, so being a kid is a great time to start inventing. And if you get your first invention patented while you're still a kid, you could end up being a kid millionaire without even having to read secret 101: How to be a kid millionaire.

PUT IT TO THE TEST:

1. FIND A PROBLEM

In fact, the more problems you can find, the better. Ask people if they face tricky or annoying problems at work or at home. Grown-ups generally have slower brains (did we say that already?), so keep on asking them. They'll eventually start noticing the problems they face on a daily basis. Remember: big problems are great – you'll be super important if you crack them. But even solving small problems will make you a hero millionaire inventor.

FUN FACT: The guy who noticed how expensive it was to have a pet cat or dog invented the pet rock and made £12 million. (Yes, it's a rock that you keep as a pet. If you still haven't killed it after a year, then you're ready for a hamster.)

2. FIND A SOLUTION

This is the easy bit, because you're a kid. Kids have creative, fresh-out-of-the-box brains that are brilliant for coming up with new ideas. We put this to the test with one of the world's most widespread problems: small kids who won't stop picking their noses. We asked some kids for the solution and they immediately said:

WHY NOT MAKE A FAKE NOSE WITH FAKE BOGEYS THAT TASTE EVEN MORE DELICIOUS THAN REAL BOGEYS?

It might sound like a pretty minor problem but it's not. Parents worry about this stuff. There are 130 million five year olds in the world, chomping away on an average of ten bogeys a day. That's 130 tonnes of bogey, every day, and over 130 million grown-ups worrying about how to stop them.

3. MAKE LOADS OF MONEY

Go the library and search for a book on how to patent your idea. A patent is a way of stopping other people from copying your invention. You send in a description of your invention to the government "Patent Office" and if they grant you a patent then no one can copy your idea.

OUR TOP-SECRET IDEA: THE PIKIT™

We made a prototype using a fake rubber nose, liquid sweets and some green food dye. Then we tested it out on a five year old. That five year old is now addicted to his pikit™ but no longer craves real bogeys. And it turns out that it's not just five year olds who pick their noses – 91 per cent of all grown-ups do it too. That's almost seven billion customers.

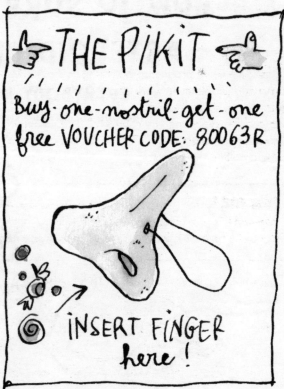

THE PIKIT

Buy-one-nostril-get-one-free VOUCHER CODE: 80063R

INSERT FINGER here!

HOW TO FIND BURIED TREASURE

EVERYBODY KNOWS:
There's a clue to some buried treasure in secret 83: How to become a secret agent. You just have to solve it.

SECRET NUMBER 36

HOW TO SURVIVE AN ASTEROID CRASH

EVERYBODY KNOWS:
No one survives an asteroid crash. Just ask a dinosaur.

DON'T ASK ME!

HOW TO BE SUPER POPULAR

EVERYBODY KNOWS:
Some people really like you, other people don't. And there's not a lot you can do about it either way.

BUT SECRET 37 IS THIS:
It's not about you. The key is to make the other person feel interesting and important. Asking people about themselves really is more interesting than talking about yourself. Think about it, what's the point of talking about yourself? You know it all already!

PUT IT TO THE TEST:
There are two KILLER SECRETS – secrets that will help make people like you in 90 seconds or less.

KILLER SECRET 1: ASK OPEN QUESTIONS
Questions come in two forms: those that open people up and those that close them down. Closed questions get a "yes" or "no" response. Open questions invite other people to talk – these usually start with "who", "when", "what", "how" and "why".

KILLER SECRET 2: ACTIVE LISTENING
Active listening means not just listening to the words coming out of the other person's mouth, but paying attention to that person's feelings as well. So how do you do this? Well, you've got to listen with much more than just your ears. And when you want to say something, remember two things:
1. Try not to interrupt the other person.
2. Enthusiastically respond to what's being said.

HOW TO TRAIN A MONKEY

EVERYBODY KNOWS:

Monkeys like bananas, so training them probably has something to do with giving them bananas.

BUT SECRET 38 IS THIS:

It would be pretty cool to have a trained monkey. It's got to be better than a hamster, right? And monkeys can do stuff that even a dog never could, such as painting, learning sign language and giving people wedgies. If you still want to know how to train a monkey, we totally understand – and we can show you how.

PUT IT TO THE TEST:

To be honest, it's pretty similar to training a dog or a parent – so do check out secret 3: How to train your parents (like a performing seal). However, there are some monkey-specific things you also need to know.

TOP MONKEY TRAINING TIPS:

1. Get a capuchin. They are the brainiest and the easiest to train. Diana monkeys and spider monkeys are second best. (Avoid marmoset monkeys at all costs.)

2. Make sure your monkey is calm. Soothe a nervous monkey by sitting next to them and speaking quietly. This will help your monkey understand that you are a source of comfort and security so they won't run off when they get nervous.

3. Use a collar and lead when your monkey is out of their cage. Take them for walks just like you would a dog. Make sure the lead is extendable with a quick release, in case the monkey gets tangled in a tree.

4. Use food. Discover your monkey's favourite food – usually not bananas. Often, they'll love mango, grasshoppers or – if you're unlucky – small rodents. Make sure to have a bag of food on you at all times. Reward your monkey with a treat immediately when they do anything right.

5. Teach your monkey sign language. Being able to talk to your monkey will take your relationship to the next level. But don't expect much. Although a gorilla can sign as well as a four-year-old human, a capuchin is more like a baby. But the process is exactly the same, so check out secret 97: How to have a conversation with a gorilla (or a baby).

HOW TO BECOME A WORLD CHAMPION

EVERYBODY KNOWS:

The chances of you becoming a world champion of anything are tiny. So don't bother trying. Just give up and watch telly instead.

BUT SECRET 39 IS THIS:

There are world championships in everything – there's bound to be something you're good at. Conkers, pea shooting, bog snorkelling, crazy golf, chess boxing, toe wrestling … you name it, there's a world championship for it.

So the chance of you becoming a world champion is actually pretty high – you just have to show up.

PUT IT TO THE TEST:

You may not be sure about toe wrestling, and neither are we (think of the athlete's foot epidemic...) but there will be something you're naturally good at. You just have to discover it. Get googling to see what world championship competitions already exist (and also where the contest for that thing is). And if you suspect you're good at something that doesn't have a world championship yet, invent one. Get your school to add it to the school summer fete, and make sure they tell the local newspaper.

If you're still stuck, then here's a bonus secret idea: at the time of writing there is (unbelievably) no World Championship for Tossing a Piece of Paper into a Bin. Here's what you need to do...

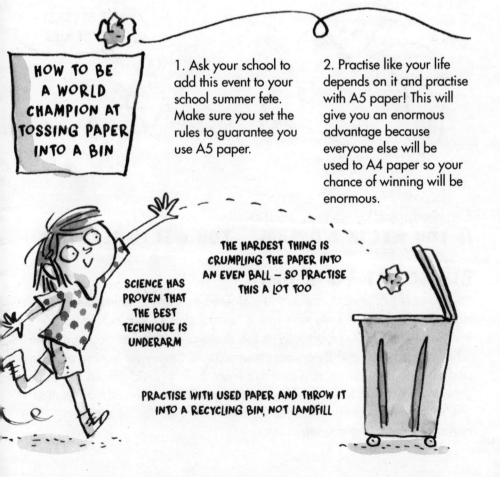

HOW TO BE A WORLD CHAMPION AT TOSSING PAPER INTO A BIN

1. Ask your school to add this event to your school summer fete. Make sure you set the rules to guarantee you use A5 paper.

2. Practise like your life depends on it and practise with A5 paper! This will give you an enormous advantage because everyone else will be used to A4 paper so your chance of winning will be enormous.

SCIENCE HAS PROVEN THAT THE BEST TECHNIQUE IS UNDERARM

THE HARDEST THING IS CRUMPLING THE PAPER INTO AN EVEN BALL – SO PRACTISE THIS A LOT TOO

PRACTISE WITH USED PAPER AND THROW IT INTO A RECYCLING BIN, NOT LANDFILL

HOW TO HAVE THE ZZZZZZ BEST DREAMS EVER

EVERYBODY KNOWS:

Dreams are stories that our brains make up while we sleep. So there's nothing you can do to avoid the bogey monster chasing you to school while your teeth fall out and everyone laughs at you for wearing your PJs.

BUT AT LEAST I DIDN'T WEE

Everybody also knows that, worst of all,

IF YOU WEE IN A DREAM ... YOU WEE IN REAL LIFE.

BUT SECRET 40 IS THIS:

You can control your dreams. You just need to learn a technique called lucid dreaming. A lucid dream feels like a normal dream, but YOU KNOW it's a dream WHILE you're actually in the dream. That means you can control what you do. You can fly across alien planets, give your enemy a wedgie, and live the impossible. Anyone can learn how to lucid dream. It's perfectly safe, easy and fun to learn. The key thing to know is this: if you realize you're dreaming in the middle of a dream, bingo! You've cracked it. You can now control the dream.

PUT IT TO THE TEST:

1. CHOOSE YOUR DREAM

A good one to start with is flying, but you can think big. What do you fancy? Riding a wolf? Fighting your PE teacher with a lightsaber? Maybe you want to learn the ukulele or invent a toy.

2. DO A REALITY CHECK

Check you're not dreaming right now by looking at your right hand. Does it look normal? Try to push a finger from your other hand through it. Doesn't work? OK, good, you're awake. In a dream, your finger poke won't feel normal – it might even pass straight through! Do this during the day, whenever you think of it (aim for 25 times a day). The more you do it, the more you'll develop a habit. The stronger the habit, the more likely you'll do the reality check when you're dreaming.

3. THINK BEFORE YOU SLEEP

As you fall asleep, think of a recent dream and something that happened in the dream that proved it was a dream. Did you fly? Were you a rock star? This is your dream-sign, the sign that you're dreaming. Now, as you're going off to sleep, think about returning to the dream. Think about noticing the dream-sign. And tell yourself "the next time I dream, I want to remember that I am dreaming". Then, as you drift off to sleep, repeat this thought in your head.

SECRET NUMBER (41)

HOW TO MASTER KUNG FU QUICKLY

EVERYBODY KNOWS:

Like all martial arts, becoming a kung fu black belt requires years of dedication, practice and effort. Unless you're a cartoon panda, in which case it just takes a few days. For humans, expect to practise for 10,000 hours before you get any good – just like everything else. During that time, you'll learn how to punch through a brick wall or how to catch a fly with chopsticks. But if you try to take short cuts, you can expect this:

BUT SECRET 41 IS THIS:

Yes, with all martial arts, you will need to train – week in, week out. BUT that doesn't mean you can't speed things up. And we mean literally speed things up. The number one thing you can do to improve your martial arts quickly is to improve your speed. That means speeding up your REACTIONS and your MOVES. For super reactions, it's easy – check out secret 42: How to get super reactions. But for the moves? You'll need to cheat.

78

PUT IT TO THE TEST:

TIME MANIPULATION:
Moving faster isn't the goal. Moving faster than your opponent expects is the goal. And for that you need to manipulate time: mix up your timings and you mix up your opponent's mind.

THINK LIKE A SNAKE:
Hypnotize your opponent by starting slow – and then suddenly switch to fast.

START SLOW

THEN FAST

MIX IT UP:
Take your favourite kung fu combination moves and mix up the speeds. Maybe start off slow, set a rhythm and then suddenly speed up. Then do the opposite. As you practise, keep changing the point where you switch speeds. Remember: if you always move at one speed, you're predictable – no matter how fast you are.

HOW TO GET SUPER REACTIONS

EVERYBODY KNOWS:

Some people are really good at sport, and the rest of us get hit in the head with the ball a lot. You've either got quick reactions or you haven't. And if your reactions are rubbish, don't even bother getting into gaming or martial arts.

BUT SECRET 42 IS THIS:

You can massively improve your reaction time just by gaming. Research proves it. And by massively faster, we mean two times faster without losing any accuracy. And there's more – because it works the other way round, too. If you want to improve your gaming or sport, then improving your reaction speed will have a big impact on how good you are.

PUT IT TO THE TEST:

1. RULER TEST
Remember the ruler test from secret 31: How to discover your hidden superpower. You can use it to measure your reactions. And over time, you can see how much you improve. And there's a bonus – even just practising the ruler test can knock a quarter off your reaction time.

2. EXERCISE
Regular exercise will improve your reaction times. Even a one-off bit of exercise can knock a third off your reaction time immediately afterwards.

3. WATER
Drinking a glass of water will typically knock a seventh off your reaction time.

4. SLEEP
Getting proper sleep (9–11 hours a night until you hit your teens) will knock a sixth off your reaction time.

5. DIET
Eating fish regularly can knock a quarter off your reaction time.

HOW TO
SOLVE A
MYSTERY

EVERYBODY KNOWS:

Children only solve mysteries in books, TV shows and movies. There's no way a child could ever really set up a detective agency and solve a proper mystery with proper baddies or treasure.

BUT SECRET 43 IS THIS:

The world is full of mysteries – just take your pick. Do you want to track down the solid gold toilet that was stolen from Blenheim Palace? Or discover Cleopatra's lost tomb? Or crack the code to the ancient language of Easter Island, and find out why they made all those big-headed statues? There are literally millions of mysteries and they all need a kid to solve them (because grown-ups have failed). In the meantime, sharpen up your Sherlock Holmes skills. Sherlock had four key powers:

MEMORY

OBSERVATION

SELF LEARNING

LOGICAL REASONING

PUT IT TO THE TEST:

You can practise your logical reasoning skills by solving one-minute mysteries. Here's one to see if you've got a particular talent for solving mysteries. Remember: only one in a hundred grown-ups can solve this.

ARE YOU A SHERLOCK?

A crime happened at Denbigh Street. The main suspect is a man named Denis Bigham. It was said that a man had been walking down the street when he was suddenly shot in the stomach. The suspect had brownish hair, bluish eyes and wore a baggy suit, just like Denis Bigham's. Denis was asked to tell the story right from the beginning.

"Well," said Denis. "I was just hanging about the park when I saw this man walking along the pathway. Suddenly, a guy came up from behind him and shot him! I ran home as fast as I could." Sherlock Holmes then asked Denis to give a description of the murderer. Denis said, "He had a red moustache, red hair and wore a baggy black suit."

"I think Denis is telling a lie," said Sherlock.

HOW DID SHERLOCK KNOW THAT DENIS WAS LYING?

Answer: The victim was shot in the stomach, so Denis Bigham must have been lying when he said he saw the victim was shot from behind.

83

HOW TO FIND A YETI (AND OTHER MYSTERY BEASTS)

EVERYBODY KNOWS:

Yetis, dragons, the Loch Ness Monster, unicorns, Mongolian death worms and other mystery creatures don't really exist. If they did, we'd have found them by now. I mean, come on, the Earth's not that big – and we have satellites and thermal-imaging cameras and stuff. Just accept it. We've found everything on Earth – if you want something new, look in space.

BUT SECRET 44 IS THIS:

Earth is still an alien planet to us – we've only explored 0.4 per cent of its total mass! The ocean floor, the upper atmosphere, the frozen bits, the jungly bits ... they have hardly been touched by explorers. And geologists are increasingly convinced that there's even a massive ocean underneath the Earth's crust, bigger than all the oceans on the surface put together. BUT that doesn't mean we're going to find the Loch Ness Monster any time soon. In fact, most of these creatures probably don't exist. Loch Ness has been swept end to end with sonar and the biggest thing in it is probably an eel.

FACT V. FICTION

RUMOURS OF MYSTERY CREATURES APPEAR ALL OVER THE WORLD.

So what's your best bet for finding a mystery beast? There's one creature that's easy to get to (if you live in the UK). Plus, you can wild camp there for free. It's the Beast of Bodmin and, best of all, IT'S ALMOST CERTAINLY REAL. How do we know? Because we've seen it...

PUT IT TO THE TEST:

I, Larry Hayes, head of the Secrets Laboratory, spotted the Beast because I was lucky. I ran out of petrol on Bodmin Moor in the middle of winter, without a phone. That might not sound lucky – but fortunately I had a packet of extra strong mints to keep me warm and awake. And so it was, as the sun rose on the morning of the 16th of January, that I saw a black cat sitting on a rock. I thought the same as you – "It's just a normal cat." So I got out of the car to take a closer look. And it ran away. So I went over to have an even closer look – and that's when I filled my pants (not literally). Because when I got over to the rock, it was actually … a massive boulder.

I didn't get a photo – and I ran back to the car without measuring any footprints or doing any sensible stuff. So there's no proof. That means it's now down to you to prove once and for all that the Beast of Bodmin is real.

HOW TO HUNT FOR THE BEAST OF BODMIN:

1. Persuade your parents that they want a free camping holiday. Both Bodmin Moor and Exmoor are open for free wild camping. Just don't forget the rules of wild camping:

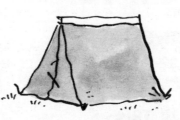

LEAVE NO TRACE

USE A STOVE, NEVER LIGHT AN OPEN FIRE

TOILET: DIG A HOLE 15CM DEEP, 50M AWAY FROM ANY WATER – AND COVER IT WITH EARTH WHEN YOU'RE DONE (INSTEAD OF FLUSHING)

2. Set up a big cat camera trap. The most fun thing would be to stay up all night. But if that's too hard, set up a camera trap.

PUT DOWN SOME MEAT

50 M

3. Take your photographic evidence to the Zoological Society.

HOW TO INVENT A JOKE

EVERYBODY KNOWS:

Only comedians invent good jokes. Other grown-ups invent corny jokes. And you're just a kid – so don't even try to invent a joke.

BUT SECRET 45 IS THIS:

Anyone can invent a joke. And, in fact, it should be on your list of 101 things to do before you become a teenager. Being funny is good for the world – even corny jokes cheer people up. And being funny is good for you – good for your health and for making friends. So how do you invent your own joke? Corny jokes are the easiest place to start because they're usually puns. A pun is a joke based on a pair of homophones – two words that sound similar but have different meanings.

AN EXAMPLE OF TWO HOMOPHONES:

BEAR   BARE

Once you've got a good pair of homophones, then it's just a question of filling out the rest of the joke.

EXAMPLE: "European" sounds a bit like "you're a-peeing". Once you've spotted that, it's easy to make up a joke by filling in some "blah, blah, blah" around it. How about:

Q. If you're French when you're drinking water in the kitchen, and Italian when you're drinking water in the living room, what are you in the toilet?
A. European.

PUT IT TO THE TEST:

1. Read through a list of homophones and near homophones.
2. Pick a pair you like.
3. Come up with a mini story or a question and answer. Remember: the best jokes put a bizarre image in people's heads. But also remember: it doesn't matter if your joke is any good. The point is, you wrote a joke! You are now a comedy hero.

FUN FACT: People have studied jokes scientifically and have discovered the world's funniest joke. It's so funny that the publisher is worried that people might stop breathing from laughing too much – so we're not allowed to publish it.

HOW TO READ SOMEONE'S MIND

EVERYBODY KNOWS:

Mind reading is just a trick. Mind readers are entertainers, or worse ... some are cheats who get gullible people to part with their cash.

BUT SECRET 46 IS THIS:

Scientists can now actually read people's minds just by looking at the pattern of activity in their brains. The bad news is that you need a massive fMRI scanner to do this, and they cost a fortune. But if your pocket money doesn't stretch to a hospital-grade brain scanner, don't worry. There's a mind reading technique that only costs 2p.

PUT IT TO THE TEST:

1. Make a pendulum using a piece of string and a 2p coin.
2. Tell a friend or family member that clockwise means yes and anticlockwise means no.
3. Ask your friend to hold the pendulum. Then ask them a question, but tell them to only answer it in their mind. If they hold that answer in their mind, the pendulum will usually begin to rotate either clockwise or anticlockwise based on their answer.

HOW TO MAKE ICE CREAM SO HEALTHY YOU CAN EAT IT FOR BREAKFAST

EVERYBODY KNOWS:

Breakfast cereal is healthy and ice cream is bad for you. And if your parents are slack enough to give you ice cream for breakfast, then all your teeth will fall out because of the sugar.

BUT SECRET 47 IS THIS:

Most breakfast cereals actually contain loads of sugar and aren't very good for you. A 49g bowl of breakfast cereal can contain loads of added sugar – about 6g, a quarter of your entire day's allowance. Added sugar is unhealthy – so just make ice cream that's got less than 6g of sugar and you're laughing.

PUT IT TO THE TEST:

Ice cream is easy if you have a freezer and a blender.

1. Ask a grown-up to blend: 400g of fruit (bananas or strawberries?) + 200ml of cream + 200ml of milk + 50g of chopped almonds.

2. Pour into a plastic tub. Then put the mixture in the freezer and eat a quarter of it the next day for breakfast.

3. Explain to your pet grown-up that this has less sugar, more fibre and more vitamins and minerals than most breakfast cereals.

HOW TO BE HAPPY

EVERYBODY KNOWS:

There are a million and one books written about "How to be happy", so obviously none of them work. Because if one did, you wouldn't need the other million. Some things will make you feel happier than others, such as reading this book. But it's OK not to feel happy all the time.

BUT SECRET 48 IS THIS:

In the last twenty years, scientists have made lots of breakthroughs in this area – including some surprising discoveries. You can't always be happy – sometimes life just sucks – but the science shows that there's always a way to make things feel better.

PUT IT TO THE TEST:

SECRET 1: DON'T TRY TO BE HAPPY

Yep, you weren't expecting that – neither were we. What the science shows is that the happiest people aren't trying to be happy – they're trying to be and do something else. They've got projects and plans and goals that they're really into. And, just as importantly, they're not afraid of feeling all the other emotions too. They're comfortable feeling sad or angry or worried – and they're comfortable telling other people when they do.

SECRET 2: GO OUTSIDE AND DO STUFF

This is the number one quick fix. Get outside every day, if you can, the earlier in the day the better. Activities with someone else are even better!

SECRET 3: MAKE SOMETHING THAT YOU LOVE

It can be literally anything. A cartoon you've drawn, a bee hotel, a mini movie, a pot of slime ... anything. When it comes to deciding what to do with your life when you leave school, aim to create something other than just money.

SECRET 4: LOADS OF OTHER STUFF

There's loads of other stuff that also helps: getting more sleep, spending time with other people, turning off tech one day a week, taking vitamin D ... the list goes on and on. But there's not enough room for us to include it all.

IMPORTANT: No one feels happy all the time and it's OK to feel unhappy. But if you are struggling, then please talk to someone about how you're feeling. Someone in your family or at school can help you. There are also charities for helping people, including children.

HOW TO RIDE AN OSTRICH

EVERYBODY KNOWS:

An ostrich is the hardest thing to ride in the known universe. It will go berserk if you try to get on its back. There's a very good reason we ride horses and not ostriches, thank you very much.

BUT SECRET 49 IS THIS:

The only reason people don't usually ride ostriches is because they don't live near ostriches. But in Dubai, children earn thousands of dollars (a day!) as ostrich jockeys. And anyone who has ever ridden an ostrich agrees that it is much more fun than riding a horse, or even a unicorn (which, despite all the hype, is just a horse with a hazardous head).

It's not just ostriches. You can ride loads of other animals, too. Not all animals, obviously – that would be ridiculous.

ANIMALS YOU CAN'T RIDE:

A DOG (YOU'LL INJURE THEIR BACK)

A GIANT SNAIL (SIZE IS RELATIVE, EVEN A GIANT SNAIL IS TOO SMALL)

A NARWHAL (OBVIOUSLY)

PUT IT TO THE TEST:

1. LEARN TO TALK OSTRICH
Communicating with an ostrich is difficult.

> **AN OSTRICH IS AS INTELLIGENT AS A 6-MONTH-OLD HUMAN BABY, SO KEEP IT SIMPLE.**

IF YOUR OSTRICH ROARS AT YOU, BACK AWAY SLOWLY – IT'S ABOUT TO KICK YOU.

2. DON'T GET KICKED
A ostrich kick is so powerful it can even kill a lion.

KEEP IT SIMPLE: OFFER AN OSTRICH FOOD AND SAY "FOOD".

3. BE THE LEADER
With an ostrich, the only sure-fire way to be the leader is to make it think you're its mum. Don't blame us if you have to feed it, change its nappy and look after it for 45 years. If you don't want to commit to being an ostrich parent, then go the feeder-leader route. Feed an ostrich for about a month and it will think you're the leader. Easy, right? Now, it's time to get on that bird!

4. GET ON, HOLD ON
Now, lift the wings and climb on from the side. Hook your legs over the ostrich's knees (which are right up high by its body). When you fall off, try to fall to one side. OK, I'm going to be completely honest, it's a bit harder than with a horse. But riding an ostrich has several distinct advantages, too.

RIDING AN OSTRICH CAN BE TRICKY. THE CONS:

BUT RIDING AN OSTRICH IS NOT IMPOSSIBLE. THE PROS:

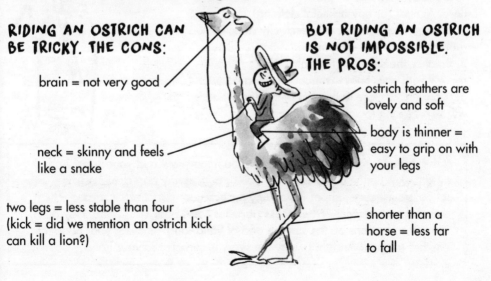

brain = not very good

ostrich feathers are lovely and soft

body is thinner = easy to grip on with your legs

neck = skinny and feels like a snake

two legs = less stable than four (kick = did we mention an ostrich kick can kill a lion?)

shorter than a horse = less far to fall

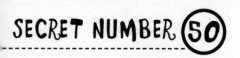

HOW TO BE PSYCHIC

EVERYBODY KNOWS:

A psychic is a person with supernatural mind powers – like seeing the future, talking to dead people and reading people's minds. One in three people have experienced psychic powers in action.

BUT SECRET 50 IS THIS:

Psychics don't really exist – they're probably just fraudsters, tricksters or entertainers. A magician, James Randi, offered $1 million to anyone who could prove their psychic abilities. Lots of people tried, but no one ever won the million. Whenever a psychic is properly put to the test, they come up short. But that doesn't mean you can't fake it too... Just take your pick – which psychic power do you want to fake? Psychokinesis (moving stuff with your mind) or telepathy (mind reading)?

PUT IT TO THE TEST:

PSYCHOKINESIS

1. Get a biodegradable plastic straw, a bottle and fleecy jumper (or any artificial clothing).
2. Charge up the straw with electricity static by rubbing it on the fleecy jumper.
3. Balance the straw on the bottle. You can now move it with your finger without touching it. Just put your finger close to the end of the straw and it will start moving towards your finger.

FUN FACT: You're basically turning both the straw and your finger into magnets! When you rub the straw you're putting tiny particles (electrons) onto it from your fleecy jumper. These tiny particles are negatively charged – like one end of a magnet. When these particles come near your hand, they push away the electrons on the surface part of your hand – turning your hand into another magnet! And that's why the straw is attracted to your hand.

FUN FACT: This next trick is based on the fact that when 9 is multiplied by any number between 2 and 9, the digits of the answer will always add up to 9. So, for example, $2 \times 9 = 18$ and if you add those digits together, $1 + 8 = 9$.

TELEPATHY

1. Ask someone to think of a secret number between 2 and 9 and then to multiply that secret number by 9. They must keep this answer, and all the following answers secret.
2. Ask them to add together the two digits of the answer. So, for example, 18 would get $1 + 8 = 9$. The big secret is that it will always be 9 no matter what number they thought of!
3. Ask them to subtract 5 from that number (they will always get 4!).
4. Ask them to match a letter to the number, based on A = 1, B = 2, C = 3 and so on (they will get D!).
5. Tell them to think of a country that begins with that letter, but not to say it out loud (they will usually choose Denmark!).
6. Now, tell them to take the second letter of that country's name and think of an animal that begins with that letter. (They will think of E and elephant!).
7. Pause and pretend to give this some thought. Then casually ask "why do you think elephants come from Denmark?"

YOU MUST BE PSYCHIC!

NOT ME!

HOW TO BLAME YOUR

EVERYBODY KNOWS:

The one who smelt it dealt it. And the one who denied it supplied it. So there's no way you can blame your fart on someone else.

BUT SECRET 51 IS THIS:

The average person farts 14 times a day. A fart is your gut's way of saying "I love you, thank you for the healthy food". And there are loads of ways to blame it on someone else.

CROP-DUSTING TECHNIQUE

The easiest way to get away with farting is the – do it on the move, like a crop-dusting plane sprays chemicals over a farm.

But if that's not possible, then you need to know how to win the blame game. First read secret 30: How to lie (and get away with it).

OK, you've done that? Good – time to check out our five-point plan for getting away with a fart. Trust us, this works. Our Secrets Laboratory can sometimes get a bit whiffy, but someone else always gets the blame.

FART ON SOMEONE ELSE

PUT IT TO THE TEST:

1. FART QUIETLY
Adjust your position to spread your bum cheeks apart.

2. FILTER IT
Fart into a cushion if you can. It will filter out the smell and slow down the spread.

3. CHOOSE A "PATSY" TO BLAME
A good patsy is someone who farts a lot – like a dog, a baby or your grandad.

4. DON'T BLAME ANYBODY
Instead, create an "aura of suspicion" by moving away from someone. Act disgusted, but don't be the first to do this – wait for someone else to react first.

5. BE UNDERSTANDING
Let the patsy get defensive, and then make them even more annoyed by being understanding and sympathetic.

WARNING! This only works if there are more than two people.

SECRET NUMBER (52)

HOW TO SCARE A GROWN-UP

EVERYBODY KNOWS:

Grown-ups are super sensible and they're not afraid of the dark. And everyone knows that teenagers are even worse. Teenagers have seen so many scary movies and they're so cool it's impossible to scare them.

BUT SECRET 52 IS THIS:

Scaring a grown-up is easy. And scaring teenagers is even easier. All you need is really dim lighting and a large mirror. If you look at yourself in a mirror in dim light for about a minute, weird stuff happens in your brain. Although scientists are not sure what produces the effect, basically, your brain gets bored so it makes up a new image. Your face in the mirror disappears or turns into something super scary.

PUT IT TO THE TEST:

1. Wait until it is dark and then pick your victim.
2. Explain that you see something scary in the mirror (the face of an old lady or wolf – you pick).
3. Get your victim to stand in front of the mirror.

4. Dim the lights down very low (a candle directly behind them is best).
5. Tell your victim to keep their head still, and count up to 60 in "Bloody Marys".
4. If their face does change into a ghost or something weird, they will probably scream and cry like a little baby. Make sure they don't knock over the candle.

If this doesn't work – you can always go for secret 100: How to scare a grown-up (cheat method).

HOW TO WIN AN ARM WRESTLE

EVERYBODY KNOWS:

The person with the long, strong arm wins an arm wrestle.

BUT SECRET 53 IS THIS:

You don't have to be the biggest or strongest to win an arm wrestle – technique can make a huge difference. The secret is all in the wrist, so maybe do some wrist-strengthening exercises first. Grab a squishy toy and follow the instructions below.

PUT IT TO THE TEST:

1. Assume the traditional arm-wrestling position.
2. Turn your palm towards your face and bend your wrist towards your shoulder. This turns your opponent's hand in the wrong direction and takes their shoulder out of the match.
3. Pull down and towards you.

For this technique to work, you still need a bit of strength – so if you're as weak as a gerbil, you need another option.

CHEAT CODE: Tell your opponent that you're going to eat a banana "for banana kid strength". Eat most of it but keep hold of a small chunk, then hide it in your cupped hand. When you start wrestling, it'll squish and feel disgusting and your opponent will instinctively pull away.

HOW TO ACE YOUR EXAMS

EVERYBODY KNOWS:

To ace your exams, you have to be born really clever. Some people are geniuses; others are good at sport, or music, or dancing, or making fart noises with an armpit. Which of these groups you fall into is probably based on your genes and there's not a lot you can do about it.

BUT SECRET 54 IS THIS:

That's a huge pile of cow dung. There's no such thing as a genius. Your brain has 100 billion brain cells with over a trillion connections. And how they're wired up is mostly down to you. So, if you want to get really good at farting with your armpit, you have to put in the practice. Don't worry, it only takes three hours tops. If you practise a bit each day, this time next week you'll be a human whoopee cushion. Exams are the same, except it will take a bit longer than a week.

SECRET 1: If you want to be good at exam questions, practise exam questions.

SECRET 2: Get in the Goldilocks zone! Don't waste your time doing stuff that's too hard or too easy. Focus on stuff that is just a bit hard. This is the Goldilocks zone – not too hot, not too cold. How do you know if you're in the Goldilocks zone? Well, if you get every fifth question wrong, that's probably about right.

SECRET 3: Practise every day. This is easier said than done. But it makes it so much easier if you can. Having some way of keeping track of how amazing you're getting will really help.

PUT IT TO THE TEST:

Does that all sound tricky? Don't worry, there's a cheat. Whether it's a maths exam, or English, or spelling there's a cheat that will help you ace your exams. You just need to access a tablet, phone or computer either at school, home or your local library.

CHEAT CODE:

Ask a grown-up to let you try an adaptive education app that adapts to you. These apps are designed to practise exam questions that are in your Goldilocks zone. So if it's too easy, they'll skip you forwards. Too hard and you'll slow down until you figure it out. Agree to use the app every day for ten minutes, in return for extra play time or screen time or sweets (so it's a win–win). Research shows that those ten minutes a day will double your learning speed. So in one year you'll make two years' progress!

TEN MINUTES A DAY

AFTER ONE YEAR

HOW TO READ SOMEONE'S MIND (AGAIN)

EVERYBODY KNOWS:

You can use the pendulum trick to do this, and it only costs 2p. See secret 46: How to read someone's mind.

BUT SECRET 55 IS THIS:

There's another way to read someone's mind that only costs 0p. It's the carrot mind-reading trick. And it's even easier.

PUT IT TO THE TEST:

1. Using an orange felt-tip (or pencil), write down the word "carrot" on a piece of paper. Fold over the paper to hide the word. Give the felt tip and paper to your friend or family member, but tell them not to look at the paper ... yet. Let them hold on to it so they know there's no cheating going on.
2. Ask them "what's 1 + 1?" and wait for them to answer. Then ask "what's 2 + 2?" and wait for them to answer. Keep going until you get to 8 + 8.
3. Finally, ask them to name a vegetable. Nine times out of ten they'll say "carrot".
4. Tell them to read the paper with "carrot" written on it. Watch them gasp. They'll totally think you're a mind reader. If you weren't feared for your mind-reading powers before, you will be now.

FUN FACT: You might be wondering: why bother with all the maths questions? The maths is just to distract their higher brain functions. When this happens, our more basic brain goes for the first thing it can think of. So the answer people usually give is "carrot" – triggered by the orange pen or pencil.

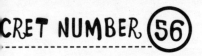

HOW TO WIN A COIN TOSS

EVERYBODY KNOWS:

There's a 50:50 chance of winning a coin toss. So there's no possible way to win every time – it's just down to luck.

BUT SECRET 56 IS THIS:

You can cheat with science on this one. There are two ways you can go.

PUT IT TO THE TEST:

CHEAT 1: PLAY THE LONG GAME

The odds of a coin toss are not 50:50! They're more like 51:49 in favour of the side facing up when you start. So call it: best out of a 100 and then always call the side that's facing up at the start.

CHEAT 2: SPIN THE COIN

If you spin the coin, instead of tossing it, then it ends up tails most of the time! It's because the heads side is heavier, so that usually falls over first.

Warning! Be careful with this one: don't catch the coin – just let it land on the floor or table.

It's all very well knowing the secret science of a coin spin – but you need to apply it to get good results. If you have a sibling, we recommend ripping this page out of the book and burying it somewhere, so they can't learn the secret. Then spin each week – best of five, loser does all the chores. You might never have to do chores again!

HOW TO MAKE UP YOUR OWN SECRET LANGUAGE

EVERYBODY KNOWS:

You can't just make up your own language – because there'd be no one talk to, so what's the point? If you want to tell your best friend that your teacher has just farted, then there's absolutely no way of doing it without writing it down and getting caught, which is really unfair because it was your teacher who farted and not you.

BUT SECRET 57 IS THIS:

Inventing a secret language is easy, and it's very handy being able to talk to your friends without grown-ups knowing what you're going on about. But first, you need to understand a bit about linguistics (the science of language) and how humans developed language in the first place, around 200,000 years ago.

LINGO FACT 1: Language developed one word at a time. Even a language with one word is useful. Some people believe that the first human word was "Aa" and it meant "Hey!" And just that one word could make a massive difference.

ONE WORD CAN BE THE DIFFERENCE
BETWEEN LIFE AND DEATH

LINGO FACT 2: Most words are a waste of breath. The world's smallest language only has 137 words, and we think you can go even lower. You can communicate most things with just twelve words – the rest are just there to give us something to do in spelling tests.

MOST WORDS CAN BE REPLACED BY THE WORD "BLAH" AND NOBODY NOTICES.

LINGO FACT 3: Children learn languages better than grown-ups. So don't wait until your brain is old – any age between 0 and 13 is best.

PUT IT TO THE TEST:

OK, to make this quick, here's a language we've invented already. Sure, you can make up your own, but if you use our version then you'll be able to talk to the millions of other kids across the planet who bought this book. Just tell all your friends they have to get this book.

First of all, you need to learn the super word. The super word is: goo. It covers every verb – or "doing" word – in the English language. For example: run, walk, climb, laugh, vom – you just use the super word, goo. After that, learn the 11 words on the next page and you can communicate just about anything.

GOO = Every verb

THEMS = Living thing

SHAP = Buy (also: sell)

NOO = No (also means: not)

ITS = Non-living thing

KEE = Know

YA = Yes (also: good!)

RUM = Power

WAA = Want

OOO = Place (also: where, here, there)

BEG = Start (also: seed, nut, egg, mum)

POO = Poop (also: fart, wee)

OK, now you just need to practise. Try translating these sentences.

Translation: Teacher did a fart and it's bad

Translation: Run

HOW TO LIFT SOMEONE UP IN THE AIR WITH JUST TWO FINGERS

EVERYBODY KNOWS:

You can't lift someone in the air with just two fingers. Unless you're a wizard, a Jedi or Matilda.

BUT SECRET 58 IS THIS:

There's a game called light as a feather, stiff as a board. And if you play it right, you can lift someone into the air.

PUT IT TO THE TEST:

1. Choose someone to die. (Not actually die – just pretend die.)
2. The chosen one lies on the floor, arms crossed over their chest.
3. Get everyone to put two fingers under the chosen one. Try to lift them and fail – because they are too heavy.
4: Call for silence. Dim the lights. Begin the ritual chant: you call and the others respond.
5. Repeat "light as a feather, stiff as a board", over and over. Every time you get to the word "light", try to lift the chosen one.
6. The chosen one will lift into the air and you'll all freak out and drop them on the floor.

FUN FACT: Chanting the rhyme together helps everybody lift at exactly the same time. That way, the person's weight is evenly spread. And we're so spooked that we forget how strong our fingers can be!

HOW TO GET OUT OF PIANO LESSONS

EVERYBODY KNOWS:

Some parents and carers force their kids to do piano lessons. This usually lasts for about one or two years, during which time everyone argues a lot about piano practice. After that period of time, the grown-ups usually give up.

BUT SECRET 59 IS THIS:

Grown-ups make you do piano lessons for one of two reasons:

REASON 1: They were forced to do piano lessons and eventually learned to play the piano.

REASON 2: They weren't forced to do piano lessons and wish they could play the piano now.

No matter which reason, there's always a way out of piano lessons.

PUT IT TO THE TEST:

PLAN A: If your parent can't play the piano say, "I'll only go to lessons if we can do it together." This should stop things pretty quickly. If they call your bluff, don't worry – they won't keep it up for long.

PLAN B: If your parent can play the piano, explain these three things to them:

80 PER CENT OF CHILDREN GIVE UP PIANO LESSONS WITHIN THE FIRST YEAR

WEEKLY ARGUMENTS ABOUT PIANO LESSONS AND PRACTICE COULD BE DAMAGING TO YOUR PARENT–CHILD RELATIONSHIP

THE NUMBER ONE REASON FOR GIVING UP IS THAT IT TAKES A LONG TIME FOR A CHILD TO FEEL THE PLEASURE TO BE HAD FROM PLAYING A SONG ON THE PIANO

HOW TO PLAY THE PIANO WITHOUT LESSONS

EVERYBODY KNOWS:

Grown-ups want the best for us. Even if piano lessons feel like torture.

BUT SECRET 60 IS THIS:

If your parents still want you to learn how to play then offer them this deal... Try a light-up keyboard for three months to see if it's "for you". Agree that if you enjoy it, you'll try lessons.

PUT IT TO THE TEST:

Light-up keyboards show you how to play songs by lighting up the keys in the right order. They let you experience playing a song and give you a feel for what it will be like to be able to play. They're also a lot of fun.

ECRET NUMBER 61

HOW TO GET SOME FREE SUGAR

EVERYBODY KNOWS

You just have to get the hiccups and then show your parent or carer secret 98: How to get rid of hiccups.

Hic
Hic

HOW TO BEFRIEND A ROBIN

EVERYBODY KNOWS:

Robins are wild birds that are scared of humans. You can't possibly have a pet robin that sits on your shoulder and eats from your hand whenever you go to the park or into your garden.

BUT SECRET 62 IS THIS:

It's easy to befriend a robin. You just need patience and worms. Pour water on some grass and collect the worms as they come to the surface. Or, easier still, buy some live mealworms from a pet shop.

PUT IT TO THE TEST:

Robins love worms. Wait until a robin is near you, then walk away from it slowly, dropping worms. After a bit, sit down and scatter more worms (including on your shoulder and leg). Do this every day or so for two weeks, and sooner or later the robin will come and sit on your leg, then your arm and shoulder. From then on, the robin will be your friend for life. It will even teach its children to be your friend. How cool is that!?!

HOW TO GET RID OF A VERRUCA

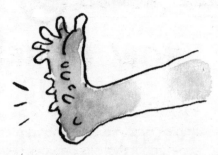

EVERYBODY KNOWS:

The only way to get rid of a verruca is by putting stuff on it, and then arguing with your parents because it's so boring, and then they threaten to take you somewhere and have it frozen off, and you scream "Noooo!" because by then your verruca feels like a friend who lives in your sock ... and so then your parents try to forget about Veronica (or whatever you've named it), AND THEN, finally, after many years and lots of screaming the verruca just disappears.

BUT SECRET 63 IS THIS:

You can get rid of Veronica just by using your mind power. A verruca is just a type of virus that lives in your foot skin. Other viruses (like colds and the flu) don't hang around for years because your immune system kicks in and kills off the virus. So why does a verruca hang around for so long? One simple reason: there's not enough blood flow to that bit of hard skin. So your immune system doesn't get a chance to do its virus-killing thing.

PUT IT TO THE TEST:

But you can increase the blood flow to your verrucary bit of foot – just by thinking it. Every night for two weeks, before you go to bed, use the super-hot finger technique but on your foot.

SUPER-HOT FOOT TECHNIQUE:

In your mind, picture having an empty body. Imagine your foot is a hot lamp. With every breath, imagine the lamp getting hotter.

HOW TO NOT BE AFRAID OF THE DARK

EVERYBODY KNOWS:

People, including kids, are afraid of all sorts of stuff. Spiders, aliens, spider-aliens ... you name it, someone's afraid of it. In fact, one in every seven teenagers has a full-on phobia, where the fear can be overwhelming.

> The big six phobias: spiders, snakes, heights, tight spaces (aka claustrophobia), dogs ... and, yes, the most common one of them all, the number one phobia, affecting one in five children, you guessed it: **THE DARK.**

BUT SECRET 64 IS THIS:

All phobias can be managed, and that includes nyctophobia, a severe fear of the dark. The secret is to build a FEAR LADDER, where you start small and gradually build up your exposure to the thing you're afraid of.

You can either do this with a parent or carer but the more you can do for yourself, the more in control you'll feel – which goes a long way when it comes to phobias and fears.

> **IMPORTANT:** However, if your phobia is so bad that it triggers panic attacks or uncontrollable anxiety, you may want to seek additional support – your GP will know what's available in your area.

PUT IT TO THE TEST:

1. BUILD A FEAR LADDER
First of all, set your goal: you want to be able to sleep with the lights off. Then work out steps to get there – start small and put in as many little steps as you can think of.

2. TALK IT THROUGH
Once you've written down your FEAR LADDER, talk it through with a grown-up. Tell them what you're planning and ask them to help.

3. LEARN RELAXATION TECHNIQUES
The big secret is: when you start to get a faster heartbeat or sweating palms, don't fight it! Stay where you are and let yourself feel the feeling. Place the palm of your hand on your stomach and breathe slooooowly and deeeeeeply. The goal is to help your brain realize you're still safe even when you're feeling panicky, because that takes the fear of fear away.

4. GO FOR IT
It's time for the first step in the ladder. The secret to success is little and often – don't wait too long between tries, and keep repeating each step until you feel comfortable to move on. And remember: you will get better at managing this fear. Over time, it will get easier and easier – but it will take time. Good luck!

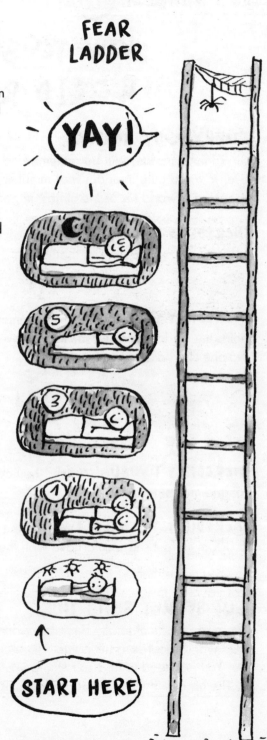

FEAR LADDER

YAY!

START HERE

HOW TO BREAK A WORLD RECORD

EVERYBODY KNOWS:

Sir Roger Bannister will be remembered through history as the first human ever to run a mile in under four minutes. But everyone also knows that breaking a world record is almost impossible unless you happen to be:

INCREDIBLY BORED: Sandeep Singh Kaila set the world record for spinning a basketball on a toothbrush.

INCREDIBLY GASSY: Bernard Clemmens holds the world record for the longest-ever fart. No one else has even come close.

INCREDIBLY UNUSUAL: Nick "the lick" Stoeberl has the world's longest tongue, measuring 10.1cm.

INCREDIBLY TALENTED: Emer McKee was 12 years old when she ran 5,000m so fast she would have won the men's Olympics in 1900.

BUT SECRET 65 IS THIS:

There are loads of totally beatable world records. Silvio Sabba has over 200 world records to his name. His secret? He picks stuff that's easy to do. You just need to find something you're a bit good at and then go for it. The hardest thing is finding out which world records are easiest to beat.

PUT IT TO THE TEST:

1. FOLLOW THE RULES

The Guinness World Records people take things very seriously. Before you even attempt the record, go to the Guinness World Records website and click on the "apply to break a record" link. Check the specific rules for your attempt (for example, skipping world records have a standard rope length) and the evidence checklist so you know exactly what you need to prove. Also check out the list of types of records that are never accepted.

2. PICK AN EASY ONE

Avoid mass-participation world records; they're a nightmare to organize. The largest-ever Conga Line had 119,986 people in it! Instead, go for something individual. Start by writing down stuff you're good at. Or, alternatively, just go for one of these – verified by the Secrets Laboratory team as officially "easy peasy".

MOST SOCKS PUT ON ONE FOOT IN 30 SECONDS
= 28 SOCKS

TALLEST TOILET PAPER TOWER IN 30 SECONDS
= 28 TOILET ROLLS

3. SMASH THAT RECORD

Just go for it! Apply well in advance – four weeks is enough time to practise most of these. So set yourself a date and stick to it.

4. IF YOU FAIL, DON'T GIVE UP

If you got close, have another go or try something else. Don't worry – even if you keep failing, you'll still eventually get a world record for the most failed attempts at a world record. And that would be the greatest world record of them all.

HOW TO BE A LEADER

EVERYBODY KNOWS:

Leaders are born,
not made.
If you look like this,
you're a born leader.
And if you don't,
don't bother.

BUT SECRET 66 IS THIS:

That's rubbish. Good leaders have five skills. Five skills that *anyone* can learn.

COMMUNICATION: Able to both explain and listen

CREATIVITY: Able to think up solutions

MOTIVATION: Wants to help and support others

POSITIVITY: Believes they'll succeed even when things are going wrong

EMPATHY: Understands what others are feeling

That might all seem like a lot, but don't worry – there's one simple trick to becoming a leader. It is remembering that good leadership is not about being "in charge", it's about supporting those you are leading. If you have that attitude, over time people will want you to be the leader.

PUT IT TO THE TEST:

Next time you're playing, don't try to take control. Instead, try to listen to what other kids want, and support them. Do this enough and you'll develop into a great leader.

LEADERSHIP GAMES

GAME 1: PASS THE HOOP

As a group, stand in a circle and hold hands. One of the people in the circle has a hula hoop around their arm. Now, try to pass that hula hoop all the way around the circle without breaking any hand-holding! To get it round, you'll need teamwork, creativity and, most importantly, communication.

GAME 2: MINEFIELD

1. Blindfold one person in the group.
2. Set up a simple obstacle course, or minefield, around them.
3. Using just four words (left, right, forwards and back), take turns guiding them through the minefield.

FORWARDS

WARNING!

Don't be tempted to use an actual minefield.

HOW TO DO IMPOSSIBLE THINGS

EVERYBODY KNOWS:

Impossible things are impossible to do. So anyone who sets out to do something impossible – like trying to eat three crackers in a minute without drinking water – is going to waste their life. You should lower your ambitions and stick to possible things, like homework and eating vegetables.

BUT SECRET 67 IS THIS:

Impossible shmimpobibble. There's no such thing as impossible. Nelson Mandela said, "It always seems impossible until it's done." And he was right. When we say "impossible", we just mean really unlikely – or really hard.

PUT IT TO THE TEST:

Repeat this mantra: "Nothing is impossible." If Beethoven could write music when he was deaf, and if Einstein could fail a school entrance exam but still become the greatest physicist who ever lived, then you can definitely do that thing with the crackers. Or whatever it is you want to do that's "impossible". There's always a way, even if you have to cheat a bit.

To get you going on your impossible dream, here are some cheat codes for common impossible things.

IMPOSSIBLE THING 1:

Eat three crackers in a minute.
Fill your mouth with water before you start, break up the crackers into little bits and slot them in your mouth bit by bit.

IMPOSSIBLE THING 2: Fold a piece of paper seven times Use an entire toilet roll. Unroll it and then fold it lengthways. If anyone complains that you've made a mess, blame it on the dog.

WHO, ME?

IMPOSSIBLE THING 3: Flick the light switch off with an elastic band without getting off the sofa. We've done this twice, so we know it's possible. But, on average, you need about 500 flicks before you get lucky. Like most things in life, patience is the key. And remember: even if you're really bad at flicking elastic bands, sooner or later there'll be a power cut at just the right moment.

EXTRA BIT: Not only are impossible things possible, it's also a good idea to have a crack at them every now and again. Failing at hard things is the secret sauce behind some of the world's most successful people. Flick through the Guinness World Records with your eyes shut and pick the record that seems the most breakable. The world record for eating baked beans with a cocktail stick is 68 in one minute. Only 68! Come on – you can beat that. See secret 65: How to break a world record. Once you've done one impossible thing, suddenly life's other challenges will feel more doable.

HOW TO GET OUT OF SCHOOL

EVERYBODY KNOWS:

You have to go to school because otherwise your parents will get in big trouble. And if you don't go, then you won't learn stuff. And you need to learn stuff so that when you grow up you can have a really cool job – like a secret agent or the person who invents a real *Jurassic Park*.

BUT SECRET 68 IS THIS:

It's easy to escape from school. But anyone who tries to write a book for kids that teaches them how to get out of school will probably find that the secret intelligence service blacks out the information because it's against national interest and would bring down civilization as we know it.

PUT IT TO THE TEST:

```
HOW TO GET OUT OF SCHOOL        TOP
                                SECRET


SUBJECT: The Great School Escape

1. ███████████ to escape ████████████ you need
is ████████████████████ Then once you are in
████████████ play it ██████ have an █████ ready
in case you ████████ teacher or grown-up. Once
you ████████████████ outside, do not ████████
██████████ from your school.
```

ECRET NUMBER (71)

ECRET NUMBER 69

HOW TO JUMP OUT OF A PLANE WITHOUT A PARACHUTE

EVERYBODY KNOWS:

Never jump out of a plane without a parachute. But if you find yourself falling out of a plane without a parachute, please write to us and we'll get right back to you.

ECRET NUMBER 70

HOW TO STOP BUTTERFLIES

EVERYBODY KNOWS:

It can feel like you have butterflies in your stomach before a school play, or a sports match, or whatever it is you're nervous about.

BUT SECRET 70 IS THIS:

Brain scans show that chewing gum dampens down stress-related information whizzing round your brain.

PUT IT TO THE TEST:

Next time you feel nervous, chew some gum or suck on a sweet. This will make you salivate, and our brains are wired to believe that we're safe whenever we're eating. More saliva means less cortisol, the stress hormone.

HOW TO RUN FASTER

EVERYBODY KNOWS:

You can either run fast or you can't. And tall people always win sports day.

BUT SECRET 71 IS THIS:

You just need to know the training secrets of the world's fastest runners. Take Usain Bolt, the world's fastest-ever person. He wasn't always fast at running. In fact, back in 1987, he was totally rubbish. He could barely walk.

USAIN BOLT
AGED 28 V. AGED 7 MONTHS

But Usain didn't let being a baby hold him back. He trained and practised. And you can learn from Usain's training secrets. You may never run 100m in 9.58 seconds but you will get faster – just by doing three things every week.

PUT IT TO THE TEST:

1. BOUNCE

Building up your quads (upper leg muscles) is the single most important thing for sprinting. Trampolining will build quads faster than anything.

BOUNCE HIGH   BOUNCE LOW   SQUATS   SKIPPING

2. VIDEO YOURSELF

To help you perfect your technique, get someone to video you while you run as fast as you can. Then watch the video and check that you are doing the following:

HEAD STILL

ELBOWS BENT

HANDS RELAXED

HANDS PUMPING FROM "HIP TO LIP"

HIGH KNEES IN LINE WITH BODY

SHORT STRIDES

3. SPRINT DRILLS

After jogging for ten minutes to warm up, do a sprint. Aim for 3m and time it. Do this timed sprint twice a week, note down your best time each week. After eight weeks, you will be amazed at how much faster you've got.

HOW TO GET JEDI MIND POWERS (CHEAT METHOD)

EVERYBODY KNOWS:

Cheating is bad, and anyone who tries to cheat their way to Jedi mind powers is probably an evil Sith Lord bent on taking over the galaxy. You should stop reading immediately before you accidentally end up on the dark side. Go back to secret 1: How to get Jedi mind powers – and do it the proper way.

BUT SECRET 72 IS THIS:

OK, you've carried on reading so we guess you must be evil. If you want to bend a metal spoon using Jedi mind powers, here's the cheat method.

PUT IT TO THE TEST:

1. Secretly bend an old teaspoon back and forth a few times. (Warning! The metal at the bend can get hot). The spoon will develop a very fine "break line" at the bend. As soon as you see that, stop. Make sure that you leave the spoon completely straight.

2. Sneak the spoon back into the kitchen. Tell everybody that you've been learning how to bend spoons with mind power.
3. Hold the spoon in one hand and ever-so-gently rub your finger over the top of the spoon.
4. In a few seconds, the spoon will bend and snap, landing on the table with a bang. The most important thing is to look as shocked as everyone else.

You now have a reputation for Jedi mind powers! From now on, your parents will be super nice to you in case you go over to the dark side.

HOW TO HAVE A CONVERSATION WITH A JELLYFISH

EVERYBODY KNOWS:

You can't have a conversation with a jellyfish. Jellyfish don't have brains, and only someone without a brain would even try to talk to one.

"KNOCK, KNOCK"

BUT SECRET 73 IS THIS:

Jellyfish use chemicals and flashing lights to communicate with each other. But no one in the history of science knows which chemicals, or what the lights mean, so if you want to discover something new to science then this could be your chance.

HEY! WHERE'S THE FOOD?

PUT IT TO THE TEST:

1. Feed the jellyfish in the dark, and always on the same side of the tank. Flash a white light three times before you put the food in.

2. After a few weeks, flash the light as normal but don't put the food in. If the jellyfish comes over for the food, you may have been the first person in the world to talk to a jellyfish.

HOW TO STOP A GROWN-UP LOOKING AT THEIR PHONE ALL THE TIME

EVERYBODY KNOWS:

Phones are great – especially if you're lost in the desert – but using one too much can be bad for you. Research has shown that people who get addicted to their phones become less fit, more stressed, more depressed and have worse sleep (making them grumpier and less fun).

FUN FACT: The typical grown-up touches their phone 2,617 times every day. Every time they check it, a brain chemical (dopamine) is released that makes them feel happy. But only for about five seconds. So then they have to check it again to get another dopamine hit.

BUT SECRET 74 IS THIS:

But you can help crack a phone addiction. First up, you need to get your parent to realize just how addicted they are. Get them to look at the digital well-being (or screen time) features on their phone. That will show them how much of their life they spend looking at their phone. Explain that cutting back on phone use will make them healthier, less stressed and better rested, so they'll have more time to play.

PUT IT TO THE TEST:

1. ONE DAY OFF

Ask your parent to pick one day a week – usually Saturday or Sunday – where they put the phone in a drawer and don't use it.

2. CHARGE IT DOWNSTAIRS

Don't let your parent charge their phone by the bed. Keeping the phone out of the bedroom will have a massive impact on their sleep, stress and general well-being. Buy an old-fashioned alarm clock if needed.

3. GET THE TECH TO HELP

Turn off all notifications. Then, set night-time settings so the phone goes black and white after 8 p.m., and finally use the digital well-being feature to set a maximum time for all their apps and favourite websites.

4. HAIR TIE TRICK

Put a hair tie across the middle of their phone. They'll still be able to answer calls but they'll be forced to rearrange the hair tie every time they use an app. This makes using the phone more mindful and acts as a constant reminder that (most of) the stuff they're doing on their phone is totally pointless.

If your parent follows all four steps, their phone use will drop dramatically. Congratulations! You now have a well-rested, fun and relaxed parent (possibly).

HOW TO BE BRAVE

EVERYBODY KNOWS:

We can't all be brave. Some people are born that way, and they're probabl\[y] foolish and will die wrestling a lion, or skateboarding off a mountain, or something that looks good on video but is really stupid. And anyway, you don't need to be brave any more – the world has health and safety regulations now.

BUT SECRET 75 IS THIS:

Brave isn't the same as fearless. In fact, you can't be brave if you don't feel fear. Being brave is feeling scared but "doing it anyway". Fear is wired into us so that we avoid dangerous situations. The problem is that while fear exists to keep us safe, sometimes it misfires and we get scared when we don't need to be.

Bravery is as important now as it ever was. Because being brave isn't just about physical courage. It's not just about being a beefy superhero who catches asteroids and throws them back out into space. There's also moral bravery – doing what you believe is right, even when it will make your life harder. And mental bravery, overcoming our fears and anxieties so you can live a fuller life.

PUT IT TO THE TEST:

It's easy to get in the habit of avoiding things that make us scared. But if you do that, then your life can get smaller and smaller and you'll miss out. But there's more to this secret because the fact is, you can get braver – a lot braver – with just a few simple tricks.

1. OWN IT

Bring your fears into the light – admit that they exist. Both to yourself and to others. You'll be amazed at how much better you feel once you've told other people about your fears.

2. IMAGINE IT

1. Think about the thing you're afraid of, while tapping into your inner superhero.
2. Take three big, deep breaths, and imagine a time you felt like you could take on the world.
3. Then think about the thing you're afraid of. Breathe into that feeling. Clench your fists for five seconds and store that feeling in them. And then let it all go – let your muscles relax with a big breath out.

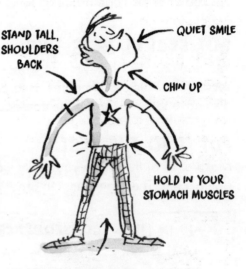

STAND TALL, SHOULDERS BACK

QUIET SMILE

CHIN UP

HOLD IN YOUR STOMACH MUSCLES

FEET APART

3. START SMALL AND BUILD BIG

For everything you find scary, there's a slightly less scary version to practise first. Scared of talking in front of a hall full of people? Do it in front of one person, then two people, and so on. And remember: building bravery is like building muscle. If you keep practising, you'll find yourself doing ever-bigger and ever-braver things. So practise stepping out of your comfort zone at least once a month. You'll be amazed at how much more powerful you'll feel.

CHEAT CODE: Feeling really nervous? Got a big test? Or a performance that you're really worried about? Try this cheat – you will immediately feel less shaky. Press your heels into the ground and take four big belly breaths. Then stretch your throat by looking up to the ceiling.

HOW TO DO WHATEVER YOU WANT

EVERYBODY KNOWS:

You can't just do whatever you want. There are laws against it. And grown-ups are generally against it (for some reason that they find hard to explain).

BUT SECRET 76 IS THIS:

Yes, you can do whatever you want – there's (usually) always a way. The secret, according to life gurus, is to prioritize and be courageous. And you also have to be aware of the consequences.

PUT IT TO THE TEST:

Make a list of the things you really want to do and the consequences of doing them. Then rank them in order of importance.

GOALS IN LIFE	CONSEQUENCES
1. Avoid school lunches	I'll probably have to make my own packed lunch every day.
2. Eat a kilo of sweets	I'll probably die of sugar poisoning.
3. Climb a mountain	I'll need to do more exercise.
4. Swim the Channel	I'll need to join a swimming club and train for years.
5. Become World President	I'll need to join a debating society and learn quantum coding so I can become a billionaire by the age of 18.

HOW TO WIN A DANCE BATTLE

EVERYBODY KNOWS:

Dance battles only happen in movies. No one has one in real life. And if by a chance you do happen to find yourself in a dance battle, you will lose unless you have spent years going to dance club or learning kung fu.

BUT SECRET 77 IS THIS:

Dance battles happen a *lot*. You've possibly even been in one without realizing it.

PUT IT TO THE TEST:

WEAPON 1:
THINK HEAD, NECK AND BODY

The big secret of brilliant dancers: their body parts are all doing ever so slightly different things in time to the music. First practise just the legs, then the arms, then the head. Then combine two at a time and finally all three elements.

WEAPON 2:
GO FUNNY OR GO HOME

You don't need to be better – you just need to be funnier. If your opponent pulls some cool moves, you will win just by copying them, badly, and pulling a funny face.

HOW TO NEGOTIATE A HIGHER PRICE WITH THE TOOTH FAIRY

EVERYBODY KNOWS:

You can't negotiate with the Tooth Fairy. You put your tooth under the pillow and you get what you're given.

LEMON SHERBET HAS EATEN AWAY AT THE BACK

The Tooth Fairy collects teeth for creepy reasons that aren't exactly clear (what would you do with 210 billion teeth?). And she sets her own prices – because, frankly, who else would buy your manky old tooth? Economists call it "a buyer's market" and the Tooth Fairy is the buyer.

FIZZY DRINK HAS EATEN AWAY AT THE BOTTOM

BUT SECRET 78 IS THIS:

You can always negotiate. Even when the other side has a much stronger negotiating position (like the Tooth Fairy). Even when the other side refuses to communicate (like the Tooth Fairy). You just need to adopt a principled negotiation strategy: aim for a fair price and a win–win deal where both you and the Tooth Fairy benefit.

THE WIN–WIN PRINCIPLE EXPLAINED:

LOSE–LOSE: GRAN AND LITTLE RED RIDING HOOD BEING EATEN + WOLF CHOPPED UP BY WOODSMAN

WIN–WIN: GRAN, WOODSMAN AND LITTLE RED SHARING THE CAKE FROM GRAN'S FOOD BASKET WITH WOLF

Next, you need to identify your BATNA (Best Alternative to a Negotiated Agreement). Unless you want to start your own manky tooth collection, your BATNA is to sell your tooth to someone else. A parent – or maybe a grandparent – might be interested in keeping one of your teeth.

PUT IT TO THE TEST:

Put your tooth somewhere safe. Then rip out this letter (or copy it out), and put it under your pillow instead of your tooth. Once communication has begun, agree to any price that is higher than your BATNA.

Dear Tooth Fairy,

I know that you usually give me £[insert usual price] for a tooth. But I am not willing to continue supply at this unfair rate. I brushed this tooth every day, twice a day, for about [insert your age] years. I believe it would be more than fair to let you have my tooth at double the usual price. Please also note that I have checked the market, and my [insert name of parent or carer] is willing to pay a lot more for my tooth than your current rate. In the interests of goodwill, I am willing to donate some of the proceeds from this tooth sale to a good cause. My preferred charity is [insert name of charity here]. Please reply by return of post. If I haven't heard from you by next week, I will seek an alternative buyer. But I am confident that with good communication we can achieve a win-win outcome.

Yours sincerely,
[Your name]

CHEAT CODE: If in doubt, turn down the Tooth Fairy's offer. You might be amazed what you're offered once you've shown you're serious about walking away from a negotiation. Or you might find out that this really is the best price you're ever going to get.

SECRET NUMBER (79)

HOW TO TRAIN A SLUG

EVERYBODY KNOWS:

Slugs are totally pointless, unless you hate lettuce – in which case they are great, because they save you from lettuce.

BUT SECRET 79 IS THIS:

Ask any gardener and they'll tell you the same thing: slugs are their NUMBER ONE ENEMY. Gardeners are fighting a war against slugs, using all the modern science and cunning at their disposal to stop them eating their lettuce. AND THE SLUGS ARE WINNING.

Slugs are winning because despite having tiny brains, they can still remember stuff, like where the lettuce is. And they teach each other too. But there may be something even more terrifying about slugs and how they learn. Scientists have discovered that the easiest way for a sea slug to learn something is to eat another sea slug. Imagine if that worked for humans. School would be a bit different...

RRRAAA

PUT IT TO THE TEST:

OK, you're not going to start feeding slugs to each other – that would be cruel. But you can test something else. Some scientists believe that slugs can pass on information just by physical contact. Yes, the theory is that you can train a slug with a hug from another slug!

HYPOTHESIS: If a garden slug touches another "trained" slug it will learn that training.

METHOD: Train a garden slug to associate mild electricity with lettuce using a simple battery circuit. It will start moving towards the electricity even when there's no lettuce! Then put the trained slug into a container with an untrained slug. Then test the untrained slug.

RESULTS:

☑ IT TOTALLY WORKED! The slug went towards the electricity.

☒ Nope, the slug went away from the electricity.

☒ Nope, the slug just sat there.

LETTUCE TRY AGAIN

If you get a positive result, you have just made a genuine scientific breakthrough.

HOW TO DROP A TOILET ROLL TUBE SO IT LANDS UPRIGHT

EVERYBODY KNOWS:

This is a weird thing to want to do. And besides, if you drop a toilet roll on its end, it just bounces over – and ends up on its side. You'd have to do it about a million times before you got lucky.

BUT SECRET 80 IS THIS:

It's actually easy – just drop the toilet roll on its side and it will bounce upright and land on its end.

PUT IT TO THE TEST:

If you want everyone to think you're amazing, do this:

1. Hold a toilet roll tube on its side, about 40cm above a table.
2. Drop it.

WARNING!
This only works once every seven tries.

BASICALLY, IT WORKS BECAUSE THE TOILET ROLL TUBE SQUASHES SLIGHTLY WHEN IT HITS THE TABLE – MAKING IT SPRINGY

AND SO IT BOUNCES UP IN THE AIR

AND AS IT COMES DOWN, THE AIR RUSHING THROUGH THE TUBE PUSHES IT UPRIGHT

HOW TO WIN A BET

EVERYBODY KNOWS:

You can't always win a bet. Some you win, some you lose.

BUT SECRET 81 IS THIS:

Yes, you can always win a bet. Try this.

PUT IT TO THE TEST:

1. Ask someone to cross their right leg over their left leg. And then rotate their right foot clockwise.

2. Tell them you can reverse the foot direction without touching them. Bet them one bazillion pounds.

ONE BAZILLION

3. Ask them to draw a number six in the air with their right finger. Their rotating foot will automatically reverse!

4. Spend the bazillion pounds on something nice.

FUN FACT: This works because your right foot and your right finger are both controlled by the left side of your brain. And it struggles to get the foot to go clockwise and the finger to go anticlockwise at the same time. If you try this with your right foot and your left finger, you'll find it much easier.

HOW TO EAT BROCCOLI

EVERYBODY KNOWS:

Grown-ups want you to eat broccoli. For some reason only known to your gran, "You need to eat your greens". And parents live by this rule. But we all know what happens when the un-stomachable vegetable hits the unavoidable plate of doom. Sometimes it's a bit bitter, and sometimes it's overcooked, soggy and tastes like a sweaty green sock. You eat a bit, you hide a bit, you complain a lot and life becomes one endless BROCCOLI DEATH MATCH.

SWEATY GREEN SOCK   BROCCOLI

BUT SECRET 82 IS THIS:

That "eat your greens" thing? Well, it turns out your gran is a nutrition genius – because there is something in it. Broccoli, in particular, is super rich in vitamins C and A and other good stuff, like fibre and antioxidants. BUT that still doesn't mean you like it.

PUT IT TO THE TEST:

There are three ways you can go with this. EMBRACE IT, AVOID IT or CHEAT. Let's see which one suits you.

TACTIC 1: EMBRACE IT

No, we haven't gone evil – if it's the taste you don't like (as opposed to the texture), then food scientists think you're only ever 16 tastes away from liking something. You just have to start small and build up over 16 meals.

1. Explain to your parents that you're going on a broccoli conversion trial. Tell them it's important to start really small – so you're not put off and sent back to square one.
2. Figure out the least disgusting way your parents cook broccoli (stir fried, boiled, steamed, whatever), then eat a tiny amount of that broccoli.
3. The next time you have broccoli – double it. Then each time after that, add another peanut-sized amount until you're up to about 16 peanuts' worth of broccoli. Then stop there, that's enough.
4. Your parents will think you're a hero, and you'll probably live for ever. But in case that doesn't work – it might be time to avoid it...

TACTIC 2: AVOID IT

OK, broccoli is not for you. We get that. The good news is that you can get all the live-for-ever-goodness that's in broccoli from other vegetables. Do you like cauliflower cheese? Explain to your parents that cauliflower has the same nutrient profile as broccoli. And if you don't like cauliflower, what about Brussels sprouts? Or kale? Or cabbage? OK, that's beginning to sound a bit desperate. Maybe it's time to cheat...

TACTIC 3: CHEAT

Smother it with ketchup.

HOW TO BECOME A SECRET AGENT

EVERYBODY KNOWS:

To qualify as a secret agent, you have to be able to jump out of a plane without a parachute while disarming a nuclear bomb with a shoelace.

BUT SECRET 83 IS THIS:

Secret agents have lots of different skills. But we've come up with just four. And you only need one of four key skills – any one of which will get you in the front door when you're over 18. But you can start building up these skills right now. And if you're strong in more than one of these skills, then you'll have a huge advantage.

WHICH ONE OF THESE SKILLS ARE YOU MOST INTERESTED IN?

FOREIGN LANGUAGES

Mandarin and Middle Eastern languages are particularly useful – but other European languages are also valuable. Remember that the younger you are, the easier it is to learn a foreign language. So start early.

COMPUTER CODING

Forget James Bond, cyber security is the most critical area for any modern intelligence service. If you like coding, then you could earn money as an "ethical hacker" while you're still at school. And once you're over 13 years old you can earn money as a "bug bounty hunter", with companies giving rewards to anyone who can break into their computer systems.

Ask a parent or carer to help you find a free online course or app to help you learn a new language or how to code.

INVESTIGATING STUFF

A good investigator notices things that others don't, has a good memory and is good at understanding complicated stuff. Check out secret 43: How to solve a mystery.

SECRET CODES

Cryptography is the study of secret codes. You need to be good at maths. Check out secret 54: How to ace your exams – it could turn you into a maths superhero.

PUT IT TO THE TEST:

Practice makes perfect. Crack this code to practise all four skills and find some real treasure that we've buried somewhere. The code is designed so that a child is more likely to solve it than a grown-up (so, grown-ups, give up now).

DAMLO X ɔWÒ ITELE TIID … / TOWARDS NUNHEAD NELSON FLYING SWEETS ARE JUST TOO MUCH FUN.HARSHAD LITTLE DUCKS COMMA DOES IT HAVE SPRINKLES THE LITTLE CREATURE ASKS-FIRST TWO INBESTIGATORS TIP BACK PLUS POINT SUPER DUPER RECTANGLE RED NOSED ONE LAUNCH SITE: 48°X GOOD LUCK AND BYE BYE.

Clue: The answer is the precise longitude and latitude for some buried silver somewhere on the planet. Each bit of text is a clue to a number. Try a search engine if you get stuck. And get your pet grown-up to follow Larry Hayes on Instagram or Twitter for extra clues.

143

HOW TO BECOME AN INFLUENCER

EVERYBODY KNOWS:
The best you can do is to watch kid millionaire influencers and get really, really jealous.

> **REMEMBER:** Most social media platforms have a minimum age of 13 – so wait until you're at least that age before setting up your own account. Before then, you can always work with a parent-or-carer-run account.

BUT SECRET 84 IS THIS:
The thing is, 99.99 per cent of people don't know the secrets of social media, so they post all the wrong stuff.

PUT IT TO THE TEST:

TIP 1: FORGET LIKES
They're worthless. Only shares count, so totally focus on shares. People share for two reasons.
1: It gives them kudos.
2: You've triggered a strong emotion.

TIP 2: KUDOS
1. Make it remarkable (think elephant's toothpaste videos).
2. Make it useful (think how-to videos).
3. Make people feel like an insider. Here's a free idea – make a video testing out each secret in this book of 101 secrets.

TIP 3: EMOTIONS ROUTE
You can go for funny, exciting, angry or, best of all, do something awe-inspiring.

TIP 4: TELL A STORY
Whatever you do, make it into a story and spread it over multiple videos.
If you're doing a video on how to train your parent, give some background.
Why do you need to train your dad?

HOW TO SURVIVE QUICKSAND

EVERYBODY KNOWS:

When you're a kid, quicksand seems like a big deal. There are zillions of movies and cartoons where people get sucked down into quicksand and are never seen again. Or they have to do clever stuff, like reach out for a jungle vine and pull themselves out.

BUT SECRET 85 IS THIS:

Quicksand is basically water-soaked sand that acts like a liquid because it's so wet. BUT it's still denser than you are – so you won't get sucked to the bottom.

PUT IT TO THE TEST:

The big risk is that the tide comes in while you're stuck. If you find yourself stuck in quicksand and near tidal water – read on.

1. Check which way the tide is going. Going out? Do step two. Coming in? Do step two fast!

2. Lie back and wriggle your legs around. This creates a small space between your legs and the quicksand into which water can flow and loosen the sand.

3. When your legs are almost free – try rolling to one side. And then keep rolling until you're clear of the quicksand.

HOW TO DISCOVER A NEW SPECIES

EVERYBODY KNOWS:

We've found just about everything there is to find on our planet, so finding a new species involves looking for aliens or at the bottom of the ocean. And both are way too expensive for the average kid.

BUT SECRET 86 IS THIS:

Scientists think there are about nine million species on Earth, but only one and a half million have been discovered. So that leaves a whopping seven and a half million species for YOU to discover. And that doesn't even include bacteria – there's probably about a trillion bacteria yet to be discovered. In fact, the chances are that there's a species of bacteria in your belly button that's completely new to science.

Sadly, there's more to it than picking out belly button fluff and saying "Found it!". To find out if your belly button bacteria are new to science, you need a lot of scientific kit and a really powerful microscope. So your best bet is to find something you can see with the human eye. Now, you could go to Loch Ness or on a yeti hunt – see secret 44: How to find a yeti (and other mystery beasts) – but we think there are easier ways to find a new species.

PUT IT TO THE TEST:

1. KNOW WHERE TO LOOK
Scientists mapping life on Earth have now taken the next step – predicting where new species are waiting to be discovered. Check out their interactive map so you know the best places to look, and what to look for. If you don't live or holiday in a hotspot, don't worry – you can still find stuff locally.

2. CATCH SOME CREATURES
Your best bet is to go for insects. There may be over five million undiscovered insect species. Also, they're easy to catch. We recommend a light trap for quick success. Try the light trap with different colours of light. Go through the rainbow and you'll see that different colours attract different insects. Use a multicolour "rainbow" torch or make your own using different colour plastic bottles.

YOU WILL NEED:

A SHEET

TENT PEGS

SOME ROPE

A TORCH

SOME STRING

A JAM JAR

3. CHECK FOR ANYTHING STRANGE
An insect book will have most of them in it, so you can quickly ignore those. If you can't find an insect in a book, take photos and use an insect ID app. Find anything that still looks a bit unusual? Send some photos to the Amateur Entomologists' Society.

IF YOU DISCOVER A NEW SPECIES,
YOU GET TO NAME IT!

HOW TO LOOK CLEVER

EVERYBODY KNOWS:

You can't look clever unless you are clever.

BUT SECRET 87 IS THIS:

You just have to wear glasses to look clever. Research has consistently shown that people with glasses are assumed to be cleverer than people without glasses. The problem is, humans have a built-in flaw: we make assumptions about people before we really know them – it's called stereotyping. Sometimes, stereotypes can be harmful. So next time you make assumptions about someone based on what they look like, remember: you're falling for the oldest mistake in the book.

PUT IT TO THE TEST:

We all have to fight against stereotypes but just occasionally you can take advantage of other people's stereotyping. Here's how:

WEAR RED Want to win at any sport? Change your kit to red. Whether it's football or the Olympics, scientists have found that the red kit wins more often than you'd expect. Probably because of the stereotype that people who wear red have more energy and strength.

WEAR BLUE Want to audition for the school play or ace an oral exam? Wear blue. Research shows that people associate blue with openness and peace, and assume that it's worn by confident people.

HOW TO GET YOUR TEACHER TO LIKE YOU

EVERYBODY KNOWS:

Teachers are similar to human beings. They have feelings, flaws and Pet Favourites. They also have Pet Hates. If you happen to be your teacher's Pet Hate, you're doomed to an eternity of misery.

BUT SECRET 88 IS THIS:

You can turn it around. By the end of *Star Wars*, even Darth Vader was likeable. And he tried to destroy half the galaxy. The secret to being likeable is having a good backstory. And your teacher will forgive you all kinds of stuff once they know your backstory.

PUT IT TO THE TEST:

It's as easy as A, B, C...
A. Think about what you do that gets your teacher really cross. For example, you talk in class too much.
B. Think about why you do that. If you don't know, speak to your parent or carer for help.
C. Once you have an idea, write it down on a card and give it to your teacher. This is your backstory!

HAPPY CHRISTMAS MR CROSSPATCH!
Thank you for helping me talk less in class. I come from a family that talks a lot all the time and so I find it really hard not to talk but your encouragement is really helping.

CHEAT CODE: If a card doesn't work, then you might want to check out secret 1: How to get Jedi mind powers – and then go over to the dark side.

HOW TO LIVE FOR EVER

EVERYBODY KNOWS:

Nothing lasts for ever. And that goes for you, too.

BUT SECRET 89 IS THIS:

Whoever first said "Nothing lasts for ever" never had to sit through maths class on a Monday morning. And they had never heard of the immortal jellyfish. It goes from adult to a baby polyp and back again, theoretically for ever.

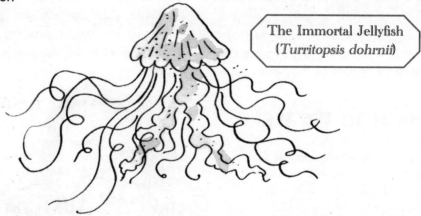

The Immortal Jellyfish
(*Turritopsis dohrnii*)

The immortal jellyfish is the only known animal capable of living for ever. All thanks to the ability of its cells to turn back into "stem cells". You can think of stem cells as baby cells that can become any type of cell – from brain cells to skin cells. But the immortal jellyfish is unique because it turns almost all of its cells back into stem cells. Imagine if your grandad turned back into an unborn baby and then started growing up all over again – well, it's a bit like that.

FUN FACT: A scientist called Shinya Yamanaka discovered a way to turn any human cell back into baby stem cells. As a result, Aubrey de Grey – English scientist and founder of the Methuselah Foundation – has said that the first immortal human has already been born.

PUT IT TO THE TEST:

To maximize your chances of still being alive when they cure old age – focus on three things: food, exercise and not dying.

1. FOOD

You can add ten years to your lifespan by eating a "Mediterranean diet" with lots of fish, olive oil, veg, fruit, nuts and pulses. Try to avoid bacon, sausages and too much added sugar. And, most importantly, avoid highly processed foods.

2. EXERCISE

You can add about seven years to your lifespan by running or exercising every day for at least 30 minutes.

3. NOT BEING KILLED

A micromort is a unit of risk that represents a one-in-a-million chance of death. Try to avoid anything too dangerous!

HOW LIKELY YOU ARE TO BE KILLED BY DIFFERENT THINGS:

SCUBA DIVING (ONE DIVE) = 5 MICROMORTS

EATING A KILOGRAM OF SUGAR (IN ONE SITTING) = 500,000 MICROMORTS

GETTING OUT OF BED FOR THE DAY (AGED 90) = 463 MICROMORTS

HOW TO NOT VOM IN A CAR

EVERYBODY KNOWS:

The only thing worse than getting carsick on long journeys is sitting next to a little sibling who does the vomming, usually on you.

BUT SECRET 90 IS THIS:

You can stop the vom.

PUT IT TO THE TEST:

Try acupressure. Gently press on your wrist with your thumb for a few minutes when you start feeling a bit barfy. The pressure point is found about three fingers below the bend in your wrist in the middle.

Go in the front. No, not the driver's seat – the other one. Being able to look ahead is a miracle cure for carsickness.

PRESS HERE! PERICARDIUM 6 ACUPRESSURE POINT – THE ONE USED FOR TRAVEL BANDS.

FUN FACT: There are more words for vomit than for any other thing in the English language, including our favourite: RALPH.

SPEW

PUKE

SICK

CHUNDER

BARF

RALPH

HOW TO MAKE SOMEONE YAWN

EVERYBODY KNOWS:

The only way to make someone yawn is to keep them up all night, probably by putting biscuit crumbs in their bed.

BUT SECRET 91 IS THIS:

You can make someone yawn just by yawning in front of them. Try it!

PUT IT TO THE TEST:

Wait until someone is looking in your direction, then yawn and see what happens. Scientists believe that the more "empathy" someone has (the ability to understand others' feelings) the more likely they are to copy your yawn. So if you yawn and another person copies you, then that person is probably quite nice.

ECRET NUMBER 92

HOW TO MAKE SOMEONE THINK ABOUT THEIR HEAD TEACHER SITTING ON THE TOILET

EVERYBODY KNOWS:

All you have to do is say, "Don't think of Mrs X on the toilet."

HOW TO MAKE ANYONE LAUGH

EVERYBODY KNOWS:

You can't make people laugh all of the time. There's no such thing as a joke so funny that everyone will laugh.

BUT SECRET 93 IS THIS:

Scientists have discovered One Universal Joke that makes almost everybody laugh. It's not the funniest joke in the world – but it works in all countries, all languages and for all ages.

PUT IT TO THE TEST:

Two ducks were sitting in a pond. One duck says, "Quack." Then the other duck says, "I was going to say that."

SECRET NUMBER (94)

HOW (NOT) TO POP A BALLOON

EVERYBODY KNOWS:

If you stick a pin in a balloon it bursts. The force on the balloon is concentrated on one tiny point so the balloon goes BANG.

BUT SECRET 94 IS THIS:

If you stick 20 pins into a balloon at the same time it doesn't burst because the force is spread out instead of being concentrated so there's not enough force to pierce the rubber.

PUT IT TO THE TEST:

1. Get twenty drawing pins and put them on a table to make a bed of nails.
2. Push the balloon onto the pins.

HOW TO DEFEAT A SUPERHERO

EVERYBODY KNOWS:

Superheroes are the good guys and so the only person reading this would be a supervillain. Which makes you a baddie, right?

BUT SECRET 95 IS THIS:

We're not telling you, baddie. Go away.

HOW TO DEFEAT A SUPERHERO WHO HAS TURNED EVIL

EVERYBODY KNOWS:

Superheroes sometimes turn evil. When this happens humans need a plan B.

BUT SECRET 96 IS THIS:

Every superhero has a weakness. They have to, or else the movie would be really boring.

PUT IT TO THE TEST:

You just need to know each superhero's particular weakness. For example, if the Hulk turns evil – just play whale song. It's one of the most soothing sounds in nature and he'll turn back into Bruce Banner. For all other superheroes-turned-evil get the Hulk to help – he's stronger than all of them.

HOW TO HAVE A CONVERSATION WITH A GORILLA (OR A BABY)

EVERYBODY KNOWS:

Gorillas only communicate by beating their chests, to say, "Go away or I will crush you, tiny human!"

BUT SECRET 97 IS THIS:

Gorillas share 98.25 per cent of our genes, which means they are our closest relatives in the animal kingdom.

KOKO THE GORILLA UNDERSTOOD 2,000 WORDS AND 1,000 HAND SIGNS. THAT'S BASICALLY MORE THAN THE AVERAGE FOUR-YEAR-OLD KID.

PUT IT TO THE TEST:

Don't use British Sign Language, use *baby* sign language – it's simpler for both gorillas and babies to do the actions. Here are some suggestions for first words to learn.

EAT

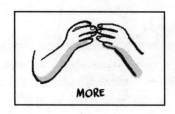

MORE

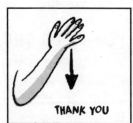

THANK YOU

HOW TO GET RID OF HICCUPS

EVERYBODY KNOWS:

To get rid of hiccups, you hold your breath and count to ten. And if that doesn't work, just wait, they'll probably go away all by themselves. The chances of you ending up like Charles Osborne are really tiny. He had hiccups for 68 years and hiccuped about 430 million times.

BUT SECRET 98 IS THIS:

There's a better way to get rid of hiccups, and it involves sugar. What's not to like? Basically, there's a nerve that runs from your stomach and guts up to your brain. It's called THE VAGUS NERVE and if you can stimulate it you can stop your hiccups. The best bit is you can stimulate the vagus nerve with sugar.

PUT IT TO THE TEST:

1. POUR A SPOONFUL OF SUGAR ON YOUR TONGUE AND LET IT DISSOLVE SLOWLY.

HIC

2. THIS TRIGGERS THE VAGUS NERVE, WHICH STOPS THE HICCUPS.

3. IF THIS DOESN'T WORK FOR SOME REASON – HEY, YOU STILL GOT SOME FREE SUGAR!

HOW TO SURVIVE BOREDOM

EVERYBODY KNOWS:
Only boring people get bored.

BUT SECRET 99 IS THIS:
You're a kid, and being a kid is never boring.

PUT IT TO THE TEST:
This book is bursting with secrets for you to try out at home or in school. You might not have a top secret Secrets Laboratory but you can still experiment with your friends and family. So stop reading this and go do something.

SECRET NUMBER (100)

HOW TO SCARE A GROWN-UP
(CHEAT METHOD)

EVERYBODY KNOWS:
You just have to prop a cushion on top of a door that's ajar and then let it fall on them when they open the door.

WARNING! Don't try this with old people.

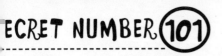

HOW TO BE A KID MILLIONAIRE

EVERYBODY KNOWS:

Hundreds of books have been written about how to become a millionaire. And indeed, publishing a book called *How to Be a Kid Millionaire* is a pretty easy way to become a millionaire.

BUT SECRET 101 IS THIS:

One of the things lots of entrepreneurs have in common is that most of them started as kids. The key is to find a problem and then solve it.

> **REMEMBER:** Grown-ups don't have a clue what's fun – and that gives you an edge. Did you know that trampolines, walkie-talkies and toy trucks were all invented by kids?!

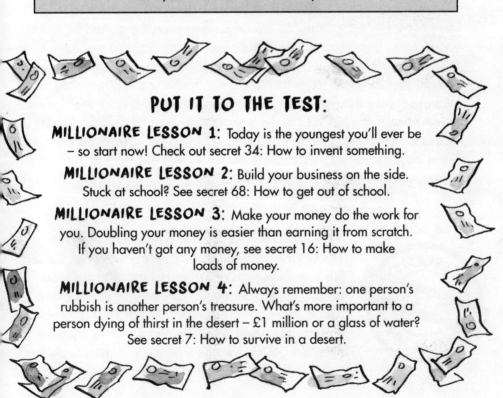

PUT IT TO THE TEST:

MILLIONAIRE LESSON 1: Today is the youngest you'll ever be – so start now! Check out secret 34: How to invent something.

MILLIONAIRE LESSON 2: Build your business on the side. Stuck at school? See secret 68: How to get out of school.

MILLIONAIRE LESSON 3: Make your money do the work for you. Doubling your money is easier than earning it from scratch. If you haven't got any money, see secret 16: How to make loads of money.

MILLIONAIRE LESSON 4: Always remember: one person's rubbish is another person's treasure. What's more important to a person dying of thirst in the desert – £1 million or a glass of water? See secret 7: How to survive in a desert.

MORE ABOUT LARRY

Larry Hayes wants to know all the answers to everything. And he wants you to know them, too. Working out of the Secrets Laboratory, Larry is now uncovering 101 more secrets. He is currently discovering how to make straight hair curly and curly hair straight, and the secret to growing taller. He has recently learned how to karate chop through a brick wall, predict the future with dreams and make a goat happy just by staring at it. He is also a future Olympic medallist, has never lost a tickle fight and can sleep like a dolphin. Larry's debut fiction book for children, *How to Survive Without Grown-Ups*, was published in 2021.

THE SECRETS LABORATORY TEAM

The wonder of writing children's books is witnessing the transformation of my verbal vomit into a work of art. Joëlle Dreidemy's humour and skill is astral. Louise Jackson's art direction has crafted a visual masterpiece. And a humble thank you to my most excellent editor, Charlie Wilson, who had to deal with wave after wave of all that vomit.